Philip Phillips

International Song Service

With Bright Gems From Fifty Authors

Philip Phillips

International Song Service
With Bright Gems From Fifty Authors

ISBN/EAN: 9783337155667

Printed in Europe, USA, Canada, Australia, Japan

Cover: Foto ©Thomas Meinert / pixelio.de

More available books at **www.hansebooks.com**

INTERNATIONAL SONG SERVICE,

WITH

BRIGHT GEMS

FROM FIFTY AUTHORS.

BY

PHILIP PHILLIPS

AND HIS SON.

FOR SUNDAY-SCHOOLS, GOSPEL MEETINGS,
MISSIONARY AND YOUNG PEOPLE'S
SOCIETIES, PRAYER-
MEETINGS,
ETC.

MAST, CROWELL & KIRKPATRICK.
NEW YORK CITY,   CHICAGO, ILL.   SPRINGFIELD,
Times Building.   Monadnock Block.   Ohio.

INTERNATIONAL SONG SERVICE.

No. 1. CORONATION SONG.
"*King of kings, and Lord of lords.*" OLIVER HOLDEN.

1. All hail the pow'r of Je-sus' name! Let angels prostrate fall; Bring forth the roy-al di - a - dem, And crown Him Lord of all; Bring forth the roy-al di - a - dem, And crown Him Lord of all.

2 Sinners! whose love can ne'er forget
  The wormwood and the gall,—
  Go, spread your trophies at His feet
  And crown Him Lord of all.
3 Ye seed of Israel's chosen race
  Ye ransomed of the fall,

Hail Him who saves you by His grace,
  And crown Him Lord of all.
4 Let every kindred, every tribe,
  On this terrestial ball,
  To Him all majesty ascribe,
  And crown Him Lord of all. Edward Perronet.

No. 2. ALL PEOPLE THAT ON EARTH.
Guillaume Franck. 1545.

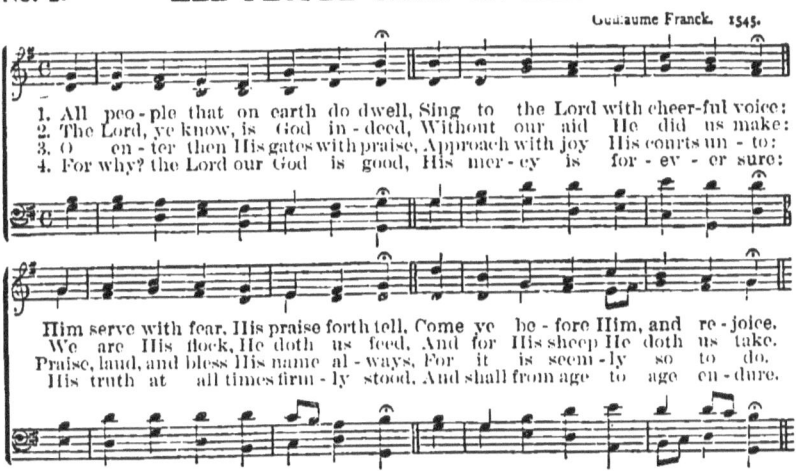

1. All peo-ple that on earth do dwell, Sing to the Lord with cheer-ful voice:
2. The Lord, ye know, is God in - deed, Without our aid He did us make:
3. O en - ter then His gates with praise, Approach with joy His courts un - to:
4. For why? the Lord our God is good, His mer - cy is for - ev - er sure:

Him serve with fear, His praise forth tell, Come ye be - fore Him, and re - joice.
We are His flock, He doth us feed, And for His sheep He doth us take.
Praise, laud, and bless His name al - ways, For it is seem - ly so to do.
His truth at all times firm - ly stood, And shall from age to age en - dure.

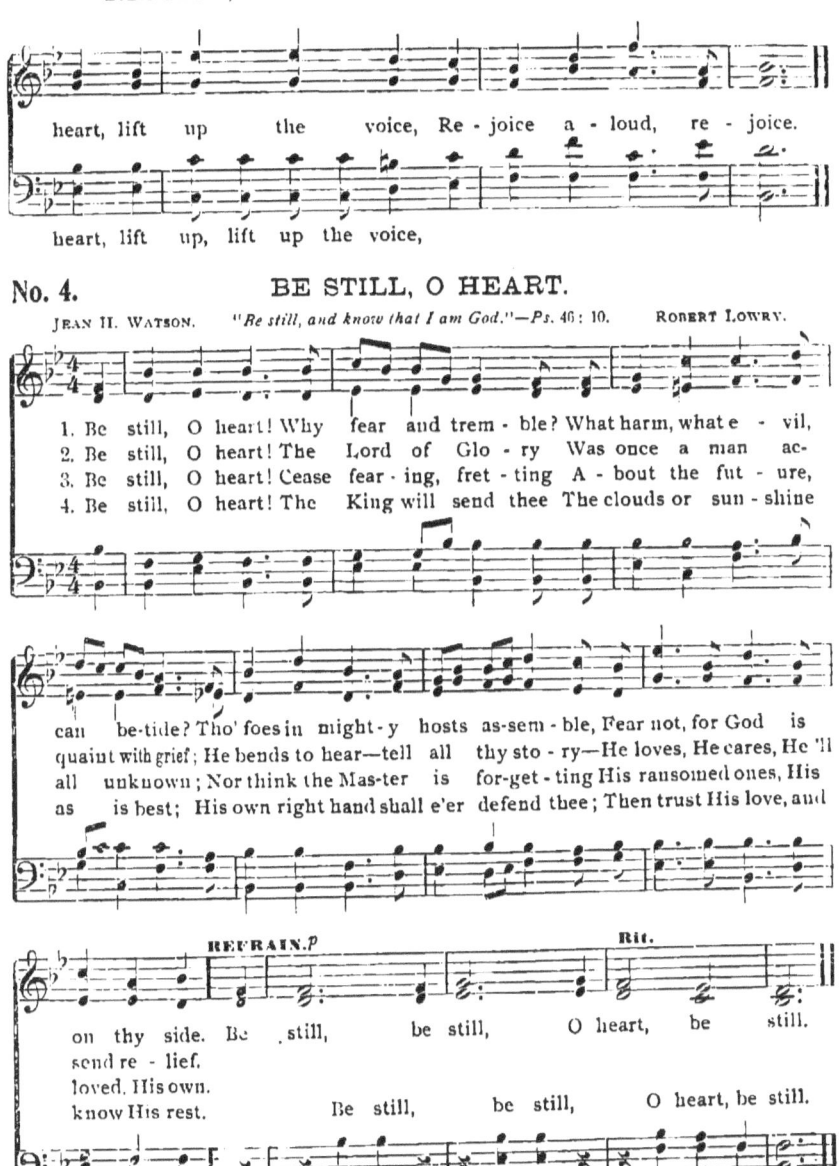

SINGING OF JESUS. Concluded.

Sing - ing, sing-ing all the day, All a-long the journey to the land above.
Sing-ing, singing,

No. 6.   GOD WILL TAKE CARE OF YOU.

FRANCES R. HAVERGAL.   *"For He careth for you."*—1 Pet. 5: 7.   ROBERT LOWRY.

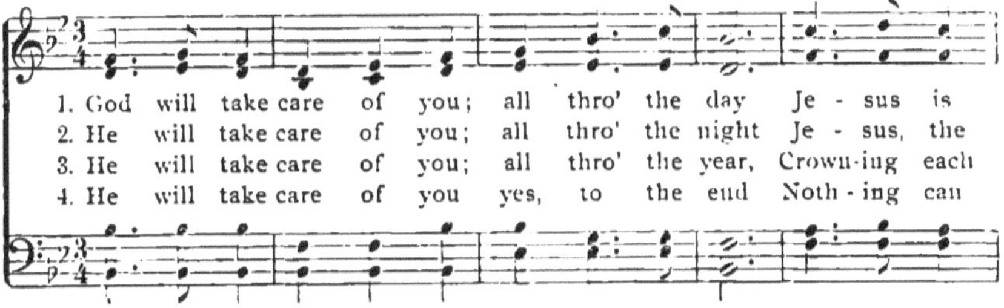

1. God will take care of you; all thro' the day Je - sus is
2. He will take care of you; all thro' the night Je - sus, the
3. He will take care of you; all thro' the year, Crown-ing each
4. He will take care of you yes, to the end Noth - ing can

near you to keep you from ill; Wak - ing or rest - ing, at
Shep - herd, His lit - tle one keeps; Dark - ness to Him is the
day with His kind - ness and love; Send - ing you bless - ings, and
al - ter His love for His own; Chil - dren be glad that you

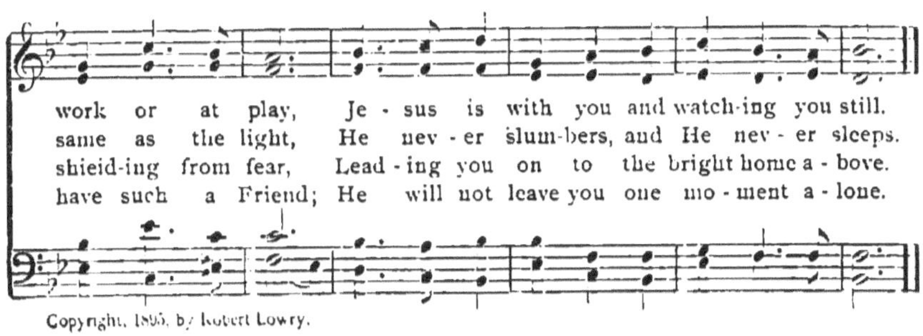

work or at play, Je - sus is with you and watch-ing you still.
same as the light, He nev - er slum-bers, and He nev - er sleeps.
shield-ing from fear, Lead - ing you on to the bright home a - bove.
have such a Friend; He will not leave you one mo - ment a - lone.

Copyright, 1895, by Robert Lowry.

PRAISE THE LORD. Concluded.

lov - ing and true, Praise ye the Lord, for He car - eth for you.

No. 8.   **LIFE IN HIS FAVOR.**

REV. JAMES YEAMS.   *"In His favor is life."—Ps. 30: 5.*   ROBERT LOWRY.

1. Life in His fa - vor! For - giv - en all sin, Sun - shine a-
2. Life in His fa - vor! The sen - tence re - pealed, Par - doned the
3. Life in His fa - vor! All else is but vain, Sin's thorn - y
4. Where can be sun-shine If night shroud the skies? Dark - ness broods

round me, and com-fort with - in; Sov - 'reign and Sav - iour, Re-
guilt - y, the sin - sick one healed; Prod - i - gal wel - comed, and
path - ways are sor - row and pain; Rich - es and pleas - ure a
o'er me un - til Thou a - rise; Ra - diance of mer - cy, ef-

deem - er and Friend, Thee will I fol - low and serve to the end.
son - ship re - stored, Hap - py the soul in the smile of its Lord!
fu - gi - tive gleam, Hon - or and splen-dor a van - ish - ing dream.
ful - gence di - vine, Sun of sal - va - tion, oh, break forth and shine!

Copyright, 1895, by Robert Lowry.

No. 9.   JESUS IS MIGHTY TO SAVE.

No. 10. ONWARD! CHRISTIAN WARRIORS.

Rev. S. F. Smith, D.D. W. H. Doane.

1. On-ward! O Chris-tian War - riors, Where-'er the trum - pet calls,
2. On-ward! with lov - ing pur - pose, Where crime and sor - row reign,
3. On-ward! the bat - tle thick - ens, The cap - tain's sig - nal see?

On-ward! the lead - er sum - mons, Be - yond the shel- t'ring walls;
On-ward! like men in earn - est, On - ward with heart and brain;
On-ward! to deeds of glo - ry, On - ward to vic - to - ry!

Onward! the work a - waits you, Fear not the cold world's frown,
Onward! to save the err - ing, To break the bonds of sin:
Onward! with God as - sist - ing, Like sol - diers true and brave,

Arm for the glo - rious con - flict, Then wear the vic - tor's crown.
On-ward! the lost to res - cue, Gems for Christ's crown to win.
Till o'er con-quer - ed for - tress, Sal - va - tions ban - ner waves.

Copyright, 1895, by W. H. Doane.

WE'RE MARCHING TO ZION. Concluded.

march-ing up-ward to Zi - on, The beauti-ful cit-y of God.

Zi - on, Zi - on,

No. 12.   I NEED THEE EVERY HOUR.

"Without Me ye can do nothing."

Mrs. ANNIE S. HAWKS.   Rev. ROBERT LOWRY, by per.

1. I need Thee ev-'ry hour, Most gra-cious Lord: No ten-der voice like Thine
2. I need Thee ev-'ry hour, Stay Thou near by; Temp-ta-tions lose their power
3. I need Thee ev-'ry hour, In joy or pain; Come quick-ly and a-bide,
4. I need Thee ev-'ry hour, Teach me Thy will; And Thy rich prom-is-es
5. I need Thee ev-'ry hour, Most Ho-ly One; Oh, make me Thine in-deed,

Can peace af-ford.
When Thou art nigh.
Or life is vain.
In me ful-fil.
Thou bless-ed Son.

REFRAIN.

I need Thee, oh, I need Thee, Ev-'ry hour I need Thee: O bless me now, my Sav-iour, I come to Thee.

No. 13. ARISE, FOR THY LIGHT IS COME

F. M. D.   FRANK M. DAVIS.

1. Give thanks and re-joice in the name of the Lord,
2. The Light of the world now il-lum-ines the way,
3. Un-fad-ing it shines, bringing peace to the soul,

The darkness of night is past; The day long for-told by the
Re-splendent, di-vine-ly bright; With love it is beam-ing from
Dis-pers-ing all fear and strife; Its rays guid-ing safe-ly the

Copyright, 1895, by Mast, Crowell & Kirkpatrick.

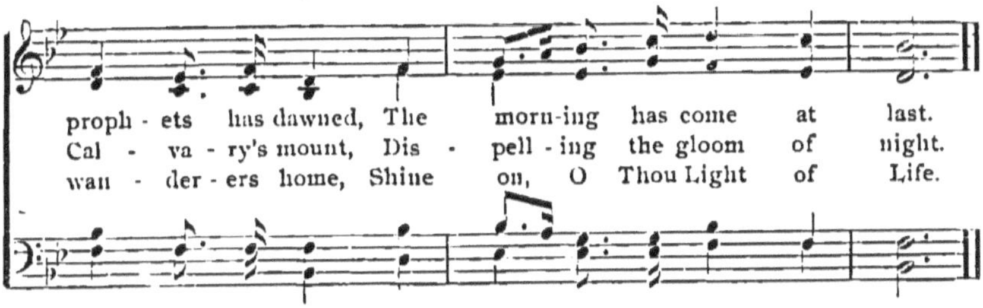

ARISE, FOR THY LIGHT IS COME. Concluded.

proph - ets has dawned, The morn-ing has come at last.
Cal - va - ry's mount, Dis - pell - ing the gloom of night.
wan - der - ers home, Shine on, O Thou Light of Life.

No. 14. THOU, WHOSE AWAKENING WORD.

A. J. SAGE, D. D.   "Let us draw near hither unto God."—1 Sam. 14: 36.   ROBERT LOWRY.

1. Thou, whose a - wak-'ning word, Stars of the morn - ing heard,
2. Thine is the glo - rious sky, Thine are the hosts on high,
3. Not with Thy thunders loud, Peal - ing thro' fire and cloud,
4. Oh, may Thy name resound The spa - cious world a - round,

And sang for joy— Spir - it of heav'n-ly grace, Draw nigh to
Thine earth and sea; Thine be this peo - ple now, Who in Thy
This tem - ple fill; But as in Beth-le - hem, When ho - ly
O'er land and sea; Till with an - gel - ic throngs, Tun - ing har -

bless the place, While pray'r and song and praise Our hearts em - ploy.
pres - ence bow, Bring - ing, with sol - emn vow, Off - 'rings to Thee.
an - gels came, Make known Thy glo - rious name, Peace and good will.
mo-nious tongues, All na - tions lift their songs In praise to Thee.

Copyright, 1895, by Robert Lowry.

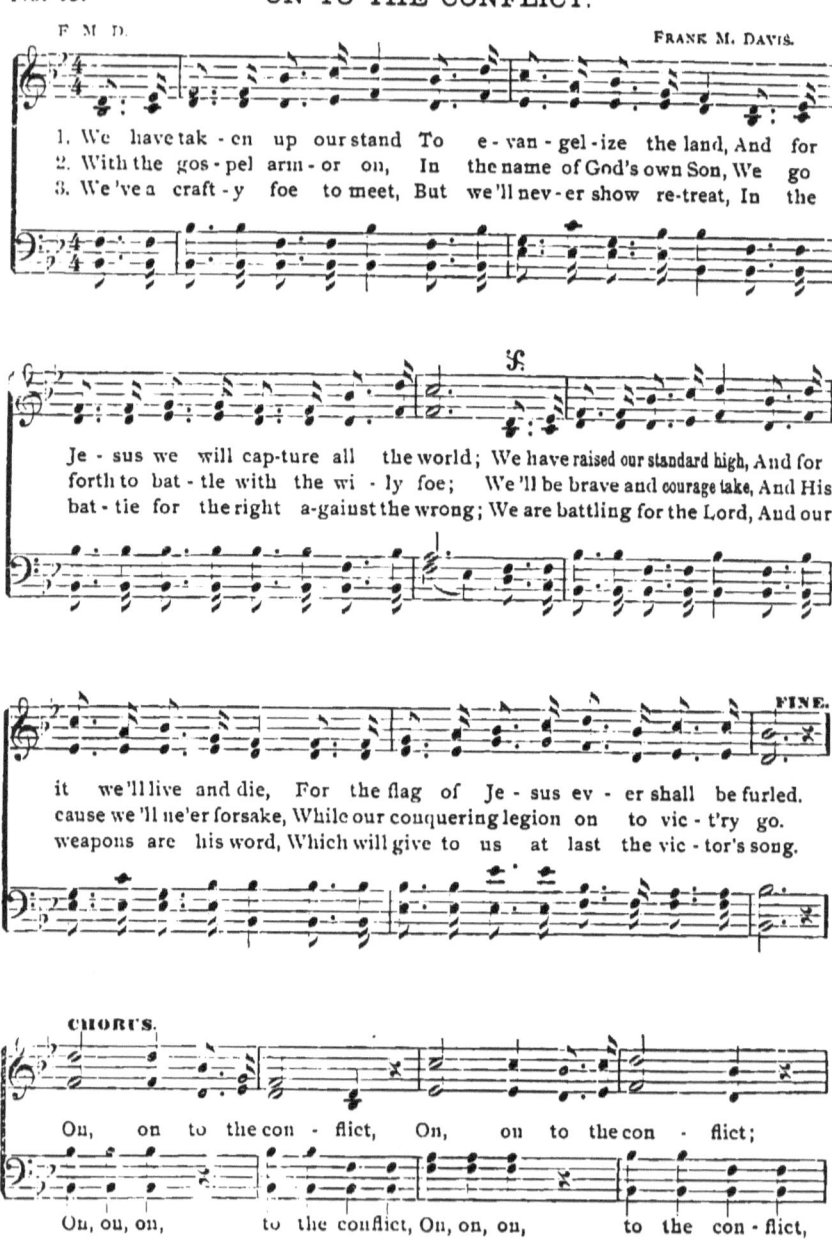

ON TO THE CONFLICT. Concluded.

Vic-to-ry, vic-to-ry, Shall our war cry be throughout the world.

throughout the world.

No. 16.   HAPPY LAND.

Old Melody.

1. There is a hap-py land, Far, far a-way, Where saints in glo-ry stand,
2. Bright, in that hap-py land, Beams ev - 'ry eye; Kept by a Father's hand,
3. Come to that hap-py land, Come, come a-way; Why will you doubting stand?

Bright, bright as day; Oh, how they sweet-ly sing, "Wor-thy is our
Love can - not die. On, then, to glo - ry run: Be a crown and
Why still de - lay? Oh, we shall hap - py be When from sin and

Sav - iour King," Loud let his prais - es ring, Praise, praise for aye!
king-dom won; And bright, a - bove the sun, Reign ev - er-more.
sor - row free; Lord, we shall dwell with Thee, Blest ev - er-more.

No. 18.   NOTHING BUT THE LOVE OF JESUS.

"Who shall separate us from the love of Christ?"—Rom. 8: 35.

ANNIE S. HANKS.   ROBERT LOWRY.

1. Noth-ing but the love of Je - sus Can sup - ply my in - most need;
2. Noth-ing but the love of Je - sus Can my longing sat - is - fy;
3. Noth-ing but the love of Je - sus Doth my wand'ring heart re - call;
4. Noth-ing but the love of Je - sus Lights the way thro' sor-row's gloom,

What tho' I have gold-en treasures? He a - lone my soul can feed.
From the fount of liv - ing wa-ters, If I drink not, I must die.
Noth-ing but His grace ex - tended Can re - store me when I fall.
Fills the bar-ren waste with singing, Makes the des - ert plac - es bloom.

CHORUS.

On - ly Je - sus, on - ly Je - sus Thro' the wil-der - ness can lead;
On - ly Je - sus, on - ly Je - sus Hears the fainting spir-it's cry;
On - ly Je - sus, on - ly Je - sus Loves me not-withstand-ing all;
On - ly Je - sus, on - ly Je - sus Breaks the si - lence of the tomb;

On - ly Je - sus, on - ly Je - sus Thro' the wil-der - ness can lead.
On - ly Je - sus, on - ly Je - sus Hears the fainting spir-it's cry.
On - ly Je - sus, on - ly Je - sus Loves me not-withstand-ing all.
On - ly Je - sus, on - ly Je - sus Breaks the si - lence of the tomb.

Copyright, '95, by Robert Lowry.

No. 22.   JESUS OF NAZARETH DIED FOR ME.

WM. H. CLARK.   WM. J. KIRKPATRICK. By per.

1. I'm help-less, Lord, to Thee I fly, In mer - cy hear me when I cry,
2. I know Thou wilt my sins for-give, For Thou hast bid me turn and live,
3. My Sav-iour now is lift - ed up, I look to Him, my on - ly hope,
4. And now I hear Thy pard'ning voice, That bids me in Thy love re-joice,

While now I urge one on - ly plea: Je - sus of Naz - a-reth died for me!
With long - ing heart I come to Thee: Je - sus of Naz - a-reth died for me!
I trust Thy word and press the plea: Je - sus of Naz - a-reth died for me!
My soul doth triumph in the plea: Je - sus of Naz - a-reth died for me!

REFRAIN.

Je - sus of Naz - a-reth died for me, Died to re-deem me and set me free.

This is my hope, my on - ly plea: Je - sus of Naz - a-reth died for me!

Copyright, 1887, by Wm. J. Kirkpatrick.

No. 23. WHO IS READY?

No. 24. THERE'S A PROMISE FROM THE LORD.

FANNY J. CROSBY.   W. H. DOANE.

1. There's a prom-ise from the Lord, Hal-le-lu-jah, 'Tis re-cord-ed in His word, Hal-le-lu-jah, That the faith-ful He'll re-ward, Hal-le-lu-jah, And that prom-ise I be-lieve, Praise His name.
2. Oh, my heart is full of song, Hal-le-lu-jah, I am sing-ing all day long, Hal-le-lu-jah, In my weak-ness I am strong, Hal-le-lu-jah, For my strength is in the Lord, Praise His name.
3. Oh, His wondrous grace to me, Hal-le-lu-jah, Shall my theme for-ev-er be, Hal-le-lu-jah, With His blood He made me free, Hal-le-lu-jah, I am hap-py in His love, Praise His name.
4. To the pal-ace gates on high, Hal-le-lu-jah, He will guide me with His eye, Hal-le-lu-jah, I shall see Him by and by, Hal-le-lu-jah, And in glo-ry at His feet Praise His name.

CHORUS.

Hal-le-lu-jah, Hal-le-lu-jah, I am trust-ing in the Lord, Hal-le-lu-jah, Hal-le-lu-jah, Hal-le-lu-jah, I am trust-ing in the Lord, Praise His name.

Copyright, 1895, by W. H. Doane.

NOT FAR FROM THE KINGDOM. Concluded.

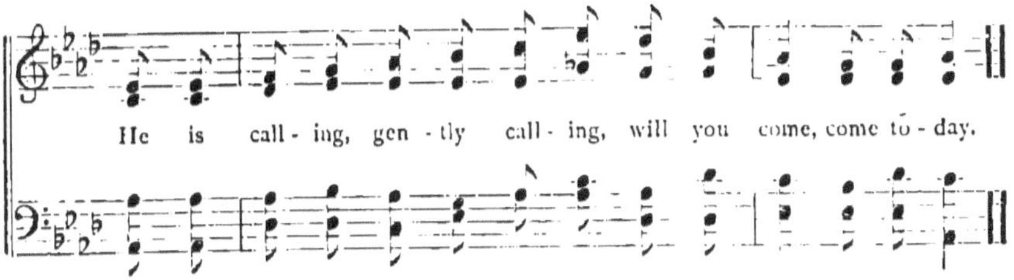

He is call-ing, gen-tly call-ing, will you come, come to-day.

No. 28. GIVE THY HEART TO ME.

FANNY J. CROSBY.   W. H. DOANE.
SOLO.

1. Hark! there comes a whis - per Steal-ing on thine ear; 'Tis the Sav - iour
2. With that voice so gen - tle, Dost thou hear Him say, Tell me all Thy
3. Wouldst thou find a ref - uge For thy soul op-press'd? Je - sus kind - ly
4. At the cross of Je - sus Let thy bur - den fall, While He gen - tly

REFRAIN.

call-ing, Soft, soft and clear.   Give thy heart to me,   Once I died for
sor-rows, Come, come a-way.
answers, I am thy rest.
whis-pers, I'll bear it all.   Just now,

thee;   Hark! hark! thy Sav - iour calls, Come, sin - ner, come.
    O come,

Copyright, 1876, by W. H. Doane.

No. 34. WE'LL WORK TILL JESUS COMES.

MRS. ELIZABETH MILLS.   DR. WM. MILLER. Arr. by W J. K.

1. Oh, land of rest for thee I sigh, When will the mo-ment come,
2. No tran-quil joys on earth I know, No peace - ful, shelt'ring dome;
3. To Je - sus Christ I fled for rest; He bade me cease to roam,
4. I sought at once my Sav-ior's side, No more my steps shall roam;

When I shall lay my ar - mor by, And dwell in peace at home?
This world's a wil - der - ness of woe, This world is not my home.
And lean for suc - cor on His breast Till He con - duct me home.
With Him I'll brave death's chill-ing tide, And reach my heav'n-ly home.

CHORUS.

We'll work, till Je - sus comes, We'll work, till Je - sus comes,
We'll work, We'll work,

We'll work, till Je - sus comes, And we'll be gath - ered home.
We'll work,

By permission.

No. 35. AT THE CROSS.

I. Watts. R. E. Hudson. By per.

1. A-las! and did my Sav-iour bleed, And did my Sovereign die?
2. Was it for crimes that I have done, He groaned up-on the tree?
3. But drops of grief can ne'er re-pay The debt of love I owe:

Would He de-vote that sa-cred head For such a worm as I?
A-maz-ing pit-y, grace un-known, And love be-yond de-gree!
Here, Lord, I give my-self a-way, 'Tis all that I can do!

CHORUS.

At the cross, at the cross, Where I first saw the light, And the bur-den of my heart rolled a-way, rolled a-way, It was there by faith

Copyright, 1885, by R. E. Hudson, Alliance, O.

AT THE CROSS. Concluded.

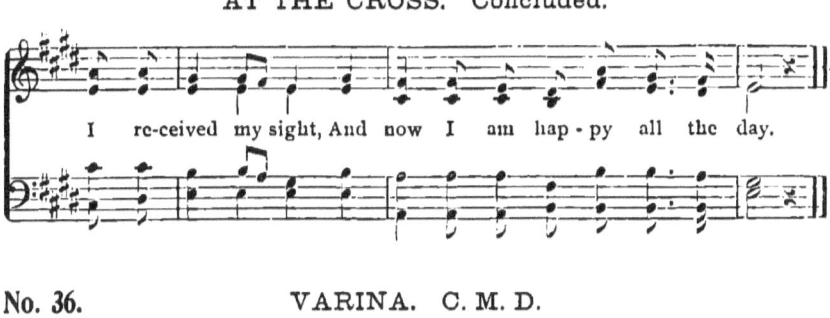

I re-ceived my sight, And now I am hap-py all the day.

No. 36. VARINA. C. M. D.

"Thine eyes shall behold the land that is very far off."

I. WATTS   GEO. F. ROOT. By per.

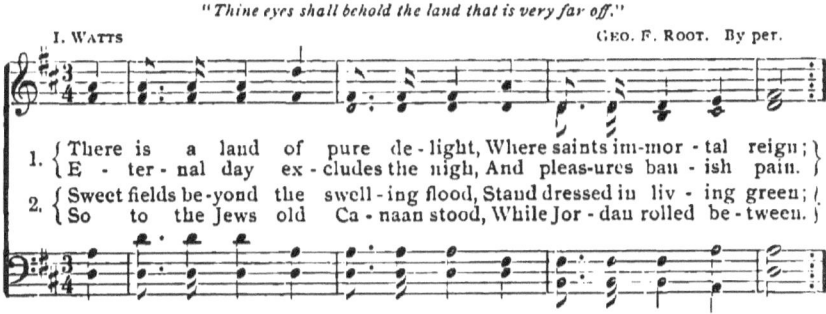

1. { There is a land of pure de-light, Where saints im-mor-tal reign;
    E-ter-nal day ex-cludes the nigh, And pleas-ures ban-ish pain. }
2. { Sweet fields be-yond the swell-ing flood, Stand dressed in liv-ing green;
    So to the Jews old Ca-naan stood, While Jor-dan rolled be-tween. }

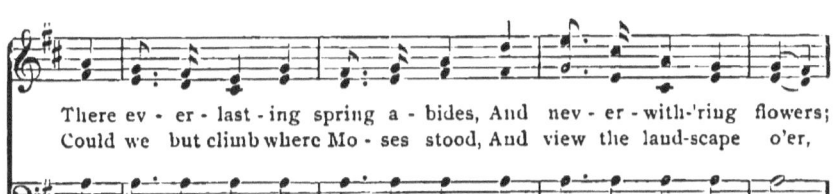

There ev-er-last-ing spring a-bides, And nev-er-with-'ring flowers;
Could we but climb where Mo-ses stood, And view the land-scape o'er,

Death, like a nar-row sea, di-vides This heav'n-ly land from ours.
Not Jor-dan's stream, nor death's cold flood, Should fright us from the shore.

No. 37. SOFTLY AND TENDERLY.

W. L. T. WILL L. THOMPSON.

By permission of Will L. Thompson & Co., E. Liverpool, O. and the Thompson Mu ic Co., Chicago, Ill.

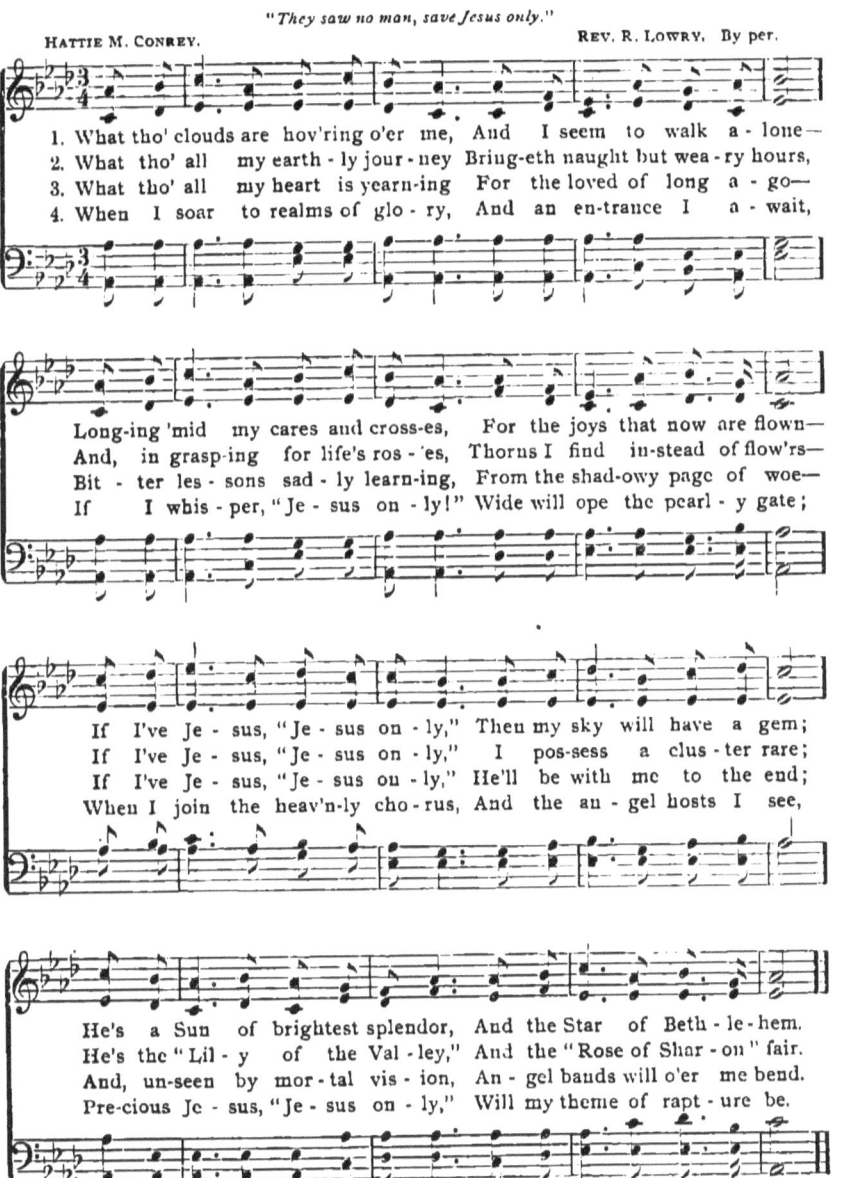

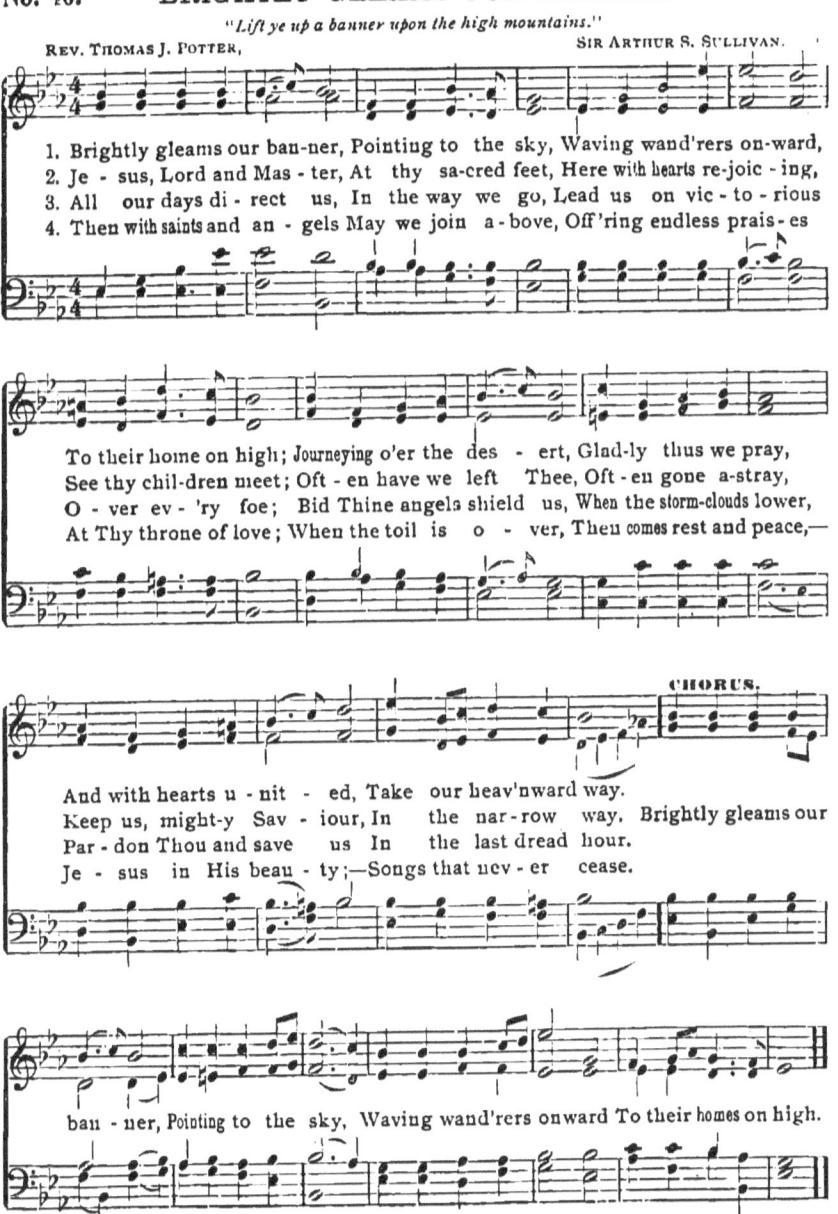

No. 41. YE MUST BE BORN AGAIN.

"Verily, verily, I say unto thee, except a man be born again, he cannot see the kingdom of God."

W. T. SLEEPER.   GEO. C. STEBBINS. By per.

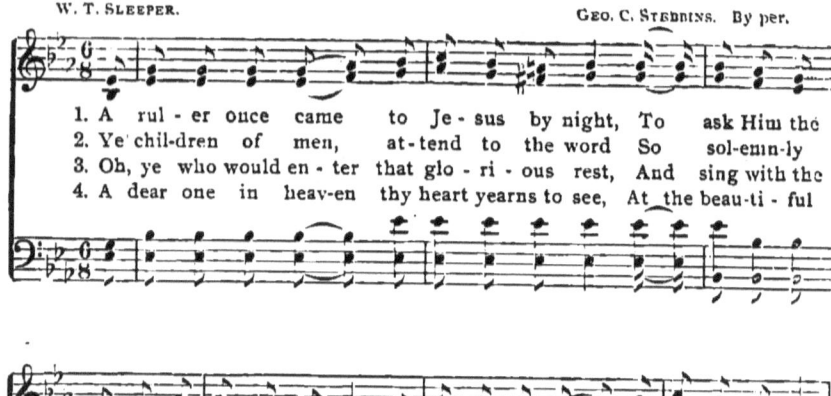

1. A rul-er once came to Je-sus by night, To ask Him the way to sal-va-tion and light;
2. Ye chil-dren of men, at-tend to the word So sol-emn-ly ut-tered by Je-sus, the Lord,
3. Oh, ye who would en-ter that glo-ri-ous rest, And sing with the ransomed the song of the blest;
4. A dear one in heav-en thy heart yearns to see, At the beau-ti-ful gate may be watching for thee;

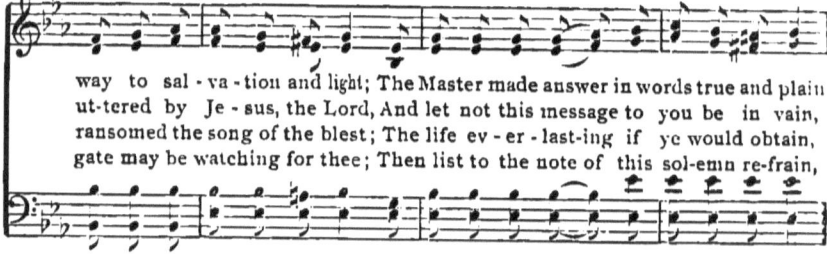

The Master made answer in words true and plain
And let not this message to you be in vain,
The life ev-er-last-ing if ye would obtain,
Then list to the note of this sol-emn re-frain,

a-gain, . . .   CHORUS.   a-

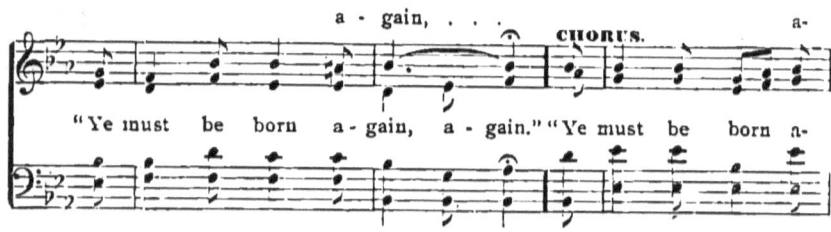

"Ye must be born a-gain, a-gain." "Ye must be born a-

gain, . . .   a-gain, . . .

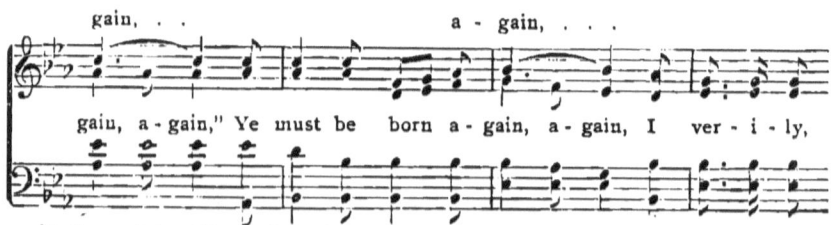

gain, a-gain," Ye must be born a-gain, a-gain, I ver-i-ly,

Used by permission of Fleming H. Revell Co., owners of copyright.

YE MUST BE BORN AGAIN. Concluded.

No. 42.   JESUS, SAVIOUR, PILOT ME.
REV. EDWARD HOPPER.   J. E. GOULD.

1. Je - sus, Sav - viour, pi - lot me, O - ver life's tem-pest-uous sea;
2. As a moth - er stills her child, Thou canst hush the o - cean wild;
3. When at last I near the shore, And the fear - ful break-ers roar

Un-known waves be - fore me roll, Hid - ing rock and treach'rous shoal;
Boist'rous waves o - bey Thy will, When Thou say'st to them "Be still!"
'Twixt me and the peace-ful rest, Then, while lean - ing on Thy breast,

Chart and com - pass come from Thee: Je - sus, Sav - iour, pi - lot me.
Wondrous Sov'- reign of the sea, Je - sus, Sav - iour, pi - lot me.
May I hear Thee say to me, "Fear not, I will pi - lot thee."

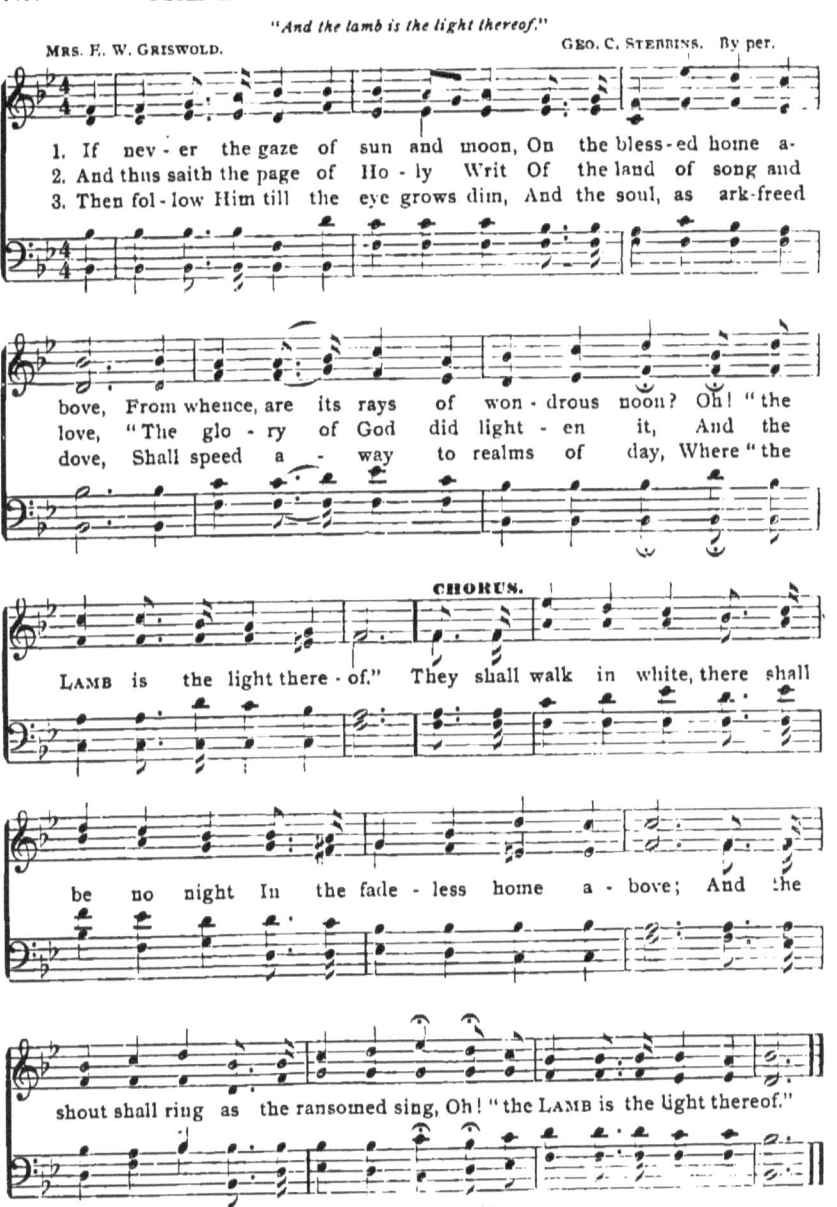

AT JESUS' FEET. Concluded.

live, For so free-ly He'll forgive, And wash all your sins a-way.

No. 46.   MORE LIKE JESUS.

FANNIE J. CROSBY.
Slow, with feeling.
W. H. DOANE.

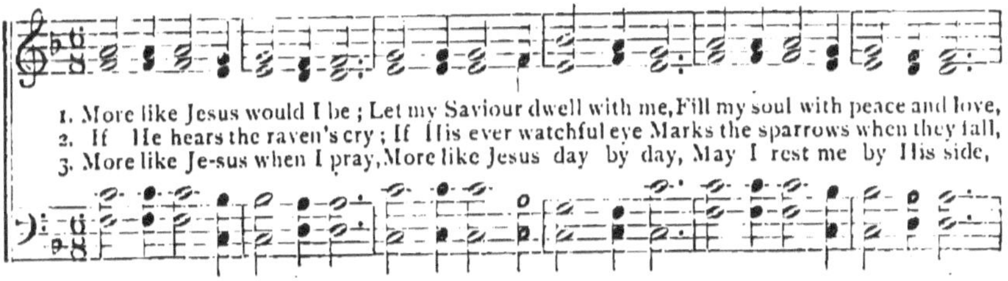

1. More like Jesus would I be; Let my Saviour dwell with me, Fill my soul with peace and love,
2. If He hears the raven's cry; If His ever watchful eye Marks the sparrows when they fall,
3. More like Je-sus when I pray, More like Jesus day by day, May I rest me by His side,

Make me gen-tle as a dove; More like Je-sus, while I go, Pil-grim in this
Sure-ly He will hear my call, He will teach me how to live, All my sim-ple
Where the tran-quil wa-ters glide; Born of Him, thro' grace renew'd, By His love my

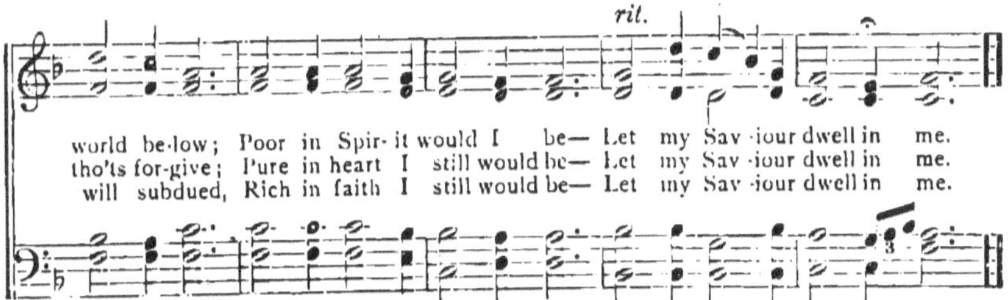

rit.

world be-low; Poor in Spir-it would I be— Let my Sav-iour dwell in me.
tho'ts for-give; Pure in heart I still would be— Let my Sav-iour dwell in me.
will subdued, Rich in faith I still would be— Let my Sav-iour dwell in me.

Copyright, 1886, by W. H. Doane.

TELL ME THE OLD, OLD STORY. Concluded.

Sto-ry, Tell me the Old, Old Sto-ry Of Je-sus and His love.

No. 48.   I AM COMING TO THE CROSS.

"Him that cometh to Me I will in no wise cast out."

REV. WM. MCDONALD.   WM. G. FISCHER. By per.

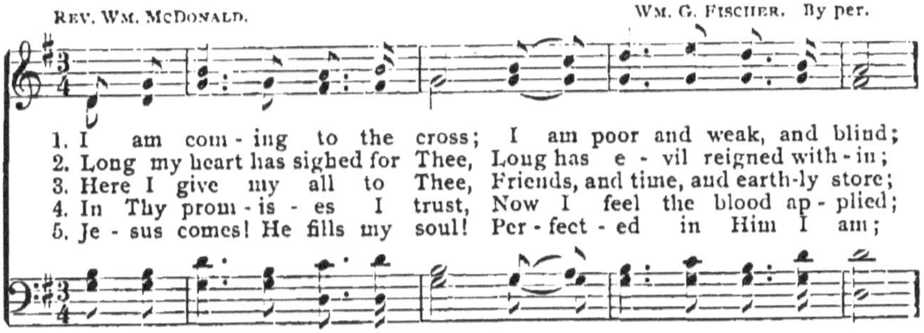

1. I am com-ing to the cross; I am poor and weak, and blind;
2. Long my heart has sighed for Thee, Long has e-vil reigned with-in;
3. Here I give my all to Thee, Friends, and time, and earth-ly store;
4. In Thy prom-is-es I trust, Now I feel the blood ap-plied;
5. Je-sus comes! He fills my soul! Per-fect-ed in Him I am;

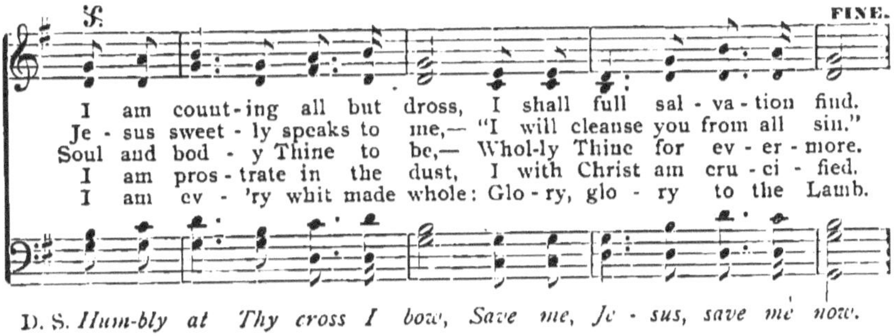

I am count-ing all but dross, I shall full sal-va-tion find.
Je-sus sweet-ly speaks to me,— "I will cleanse you from all sin."
Soul and bod-y Thine to be,— Whol-ly Thine for ev-er-more.
I am pros-trate in the dust, I with Christ am cru-ci-fied.
I am ev-'ry whit made whole: Glo-ry, glo-ry to the Lamb.

D. S. *Hum-bly at Thy cross I bow, Save me, Je-sus, save me now.*

CHORUS.

I am trust-ing, Lord, in Thee, Blest Lamb of Cal-va-ry;

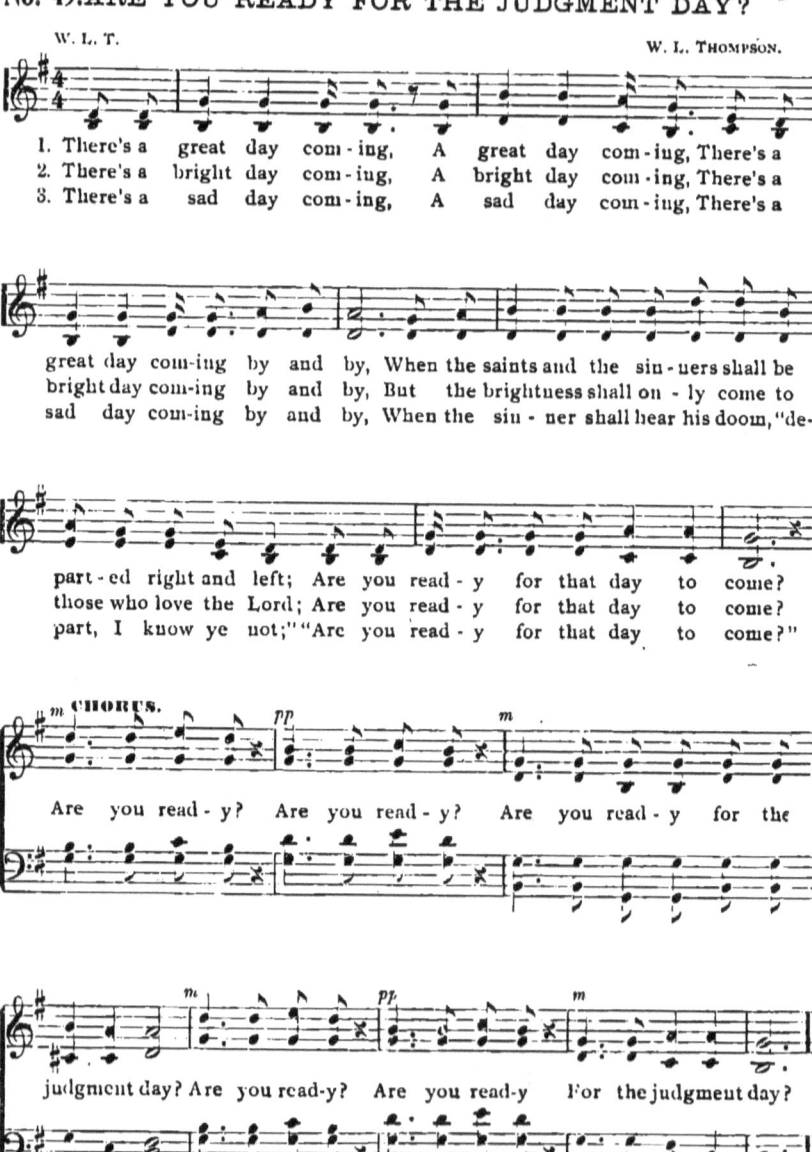

JESUS CALLS THEE. Concluded.

Call-ing ten-der-ly, call-ing lov-ing-ly, "Come, O sin-ner, come."

No. 52. HALF HAS NEVER YET BEEN TOLD.

FRANCES RIDLEY HAVERGAL. R. E. HUDSON. By per.

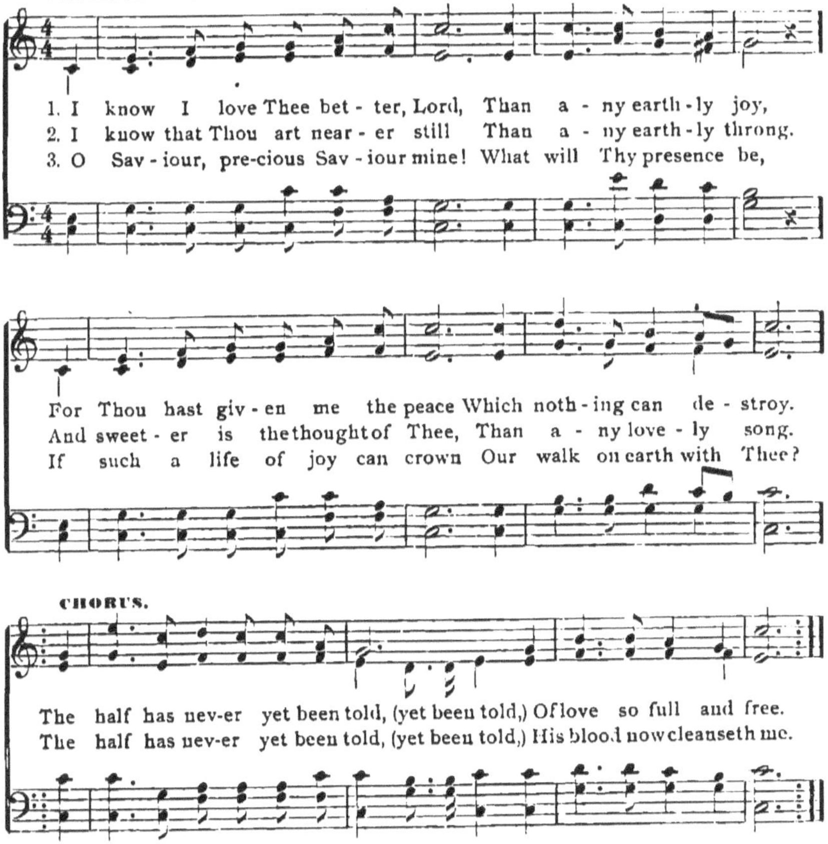

1. I know I love Thee bet-ter, Lord, Than a-ny earth-ly joy,
2. I know that Thou art near-er still Than a-ny earth-ly throng.
3. O Sav-iour, pre-cious Sav-iour mine! What will Thy presence be,

For Thou hast giv-en me the peace Which noth-ing can de-stroy.
And sweet-er is the thought of Thee, Than a-ny love-ly song.
If such a life of joy can crown Our walk on earth with Thee?

CHORUS.

The half has nev-er yet been told, (yet been told,) Of love so full and free.
The half has nev-er yet been told, (yet been told,) His blood now cleanseth me.

Copyright, 1881, by R. E. Hudson, Alliance, O.

No. 55. WILL JESUS FIND US WATCHING?

'Watch therefore; for ye know not what hour your Lord doth come.'

FANNY J. CROSBY.   W. H. DOANE. By per.

1. When Je-sus comes to re-ward His ser-vants, Whether it be
2. If at the dawn of the ear-ly morn-ing, He shall call us
3. Have we been true to the trust He left us? Do we seek to
4. Bless-ed are those whom the Lord finds watch-ing, In His glo-ry

noon or night, Faith-ful to Him will He find us watch-ing,
one by one, When to the Lord we re-store our tal-ents,
do our best? If in our hearts there is naught con-demns us,
they shall share; If He shall come at the dawn-or mid-night,

Rit.   **REFRAIN.**

With our lamps all trimm'd and bright?
Will He an-swer thee— Well done?   Oh, can we say we are
We shall have a glo-rious rest.
Will He find us watch-ing there.

read-y, broth-er, Read-y for the soul's bright home? Say will He

WILL JESUS FIND US WATCHING? Concluded.

find you and me still watching, Wait-ing, wait-ing when the Lord shall come?

No. 56. NOTHING BUT LEAVES.

"And when He came to it He found nothing but leaves."

LUCY EVELINA AKERMAN. SILAS J. VAIL. By per.

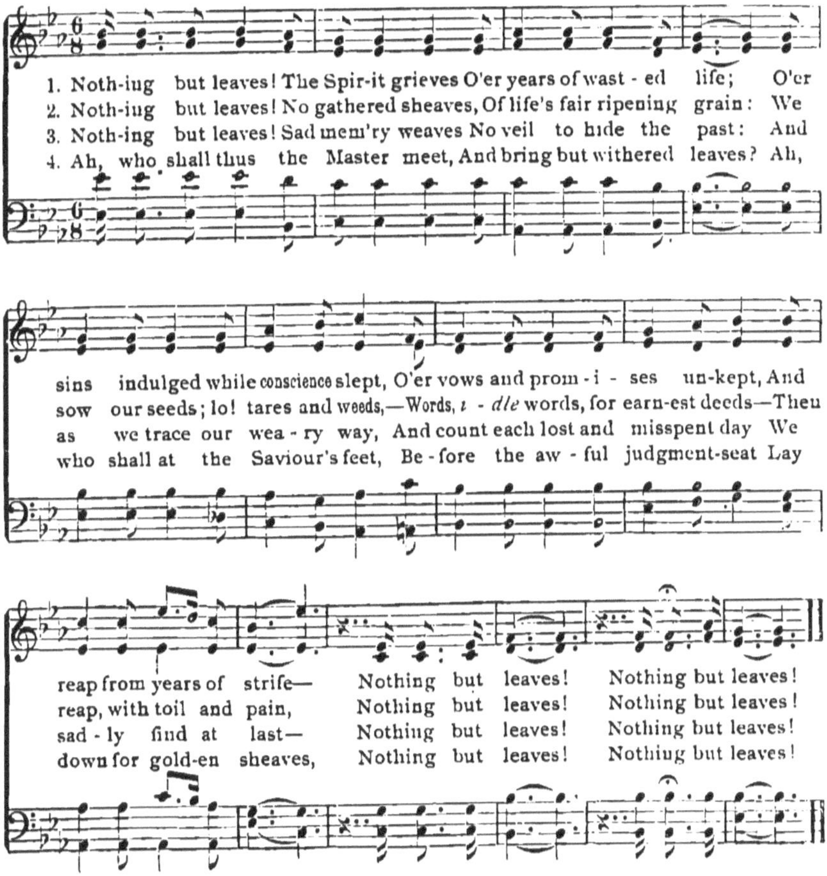

1. Noth-ing but leaves! The Spir-it grieves O'er years of wast-ed life; O'er
2. Noth-ing but leaves! No gathered sheaves, Of life's fair ripening grain: We
3. Noth-ing but leaves! Sad mem'ry weaves No veil to hide the past: And
4. Ah, who shall thus the Master meet, And bring but withered leaves? Ah,

sins indulged while conscience slept, O'er vows and prom-i-ses un-kept, And
sow our seeds; lo! tares and weeds,—Words, i-dle words, for earn-est deeds—Then
as we trace our wea-ry way, And count each lost and misspent day We
who shall at the Saviour's feet, Be-fore the aw-ful judgment-seat Lay

reap from years of strife—   Nothing but leaves!   Nothing but leaves!
reap, with toil and pain,   Nothing but leaves!   Nothing but leaves!
sad-ly find at last—   Nothing but leaves!   Nothing but leaves!
down for gold-en sheaves,   Nothing but leaves!   Nothing but leaves!

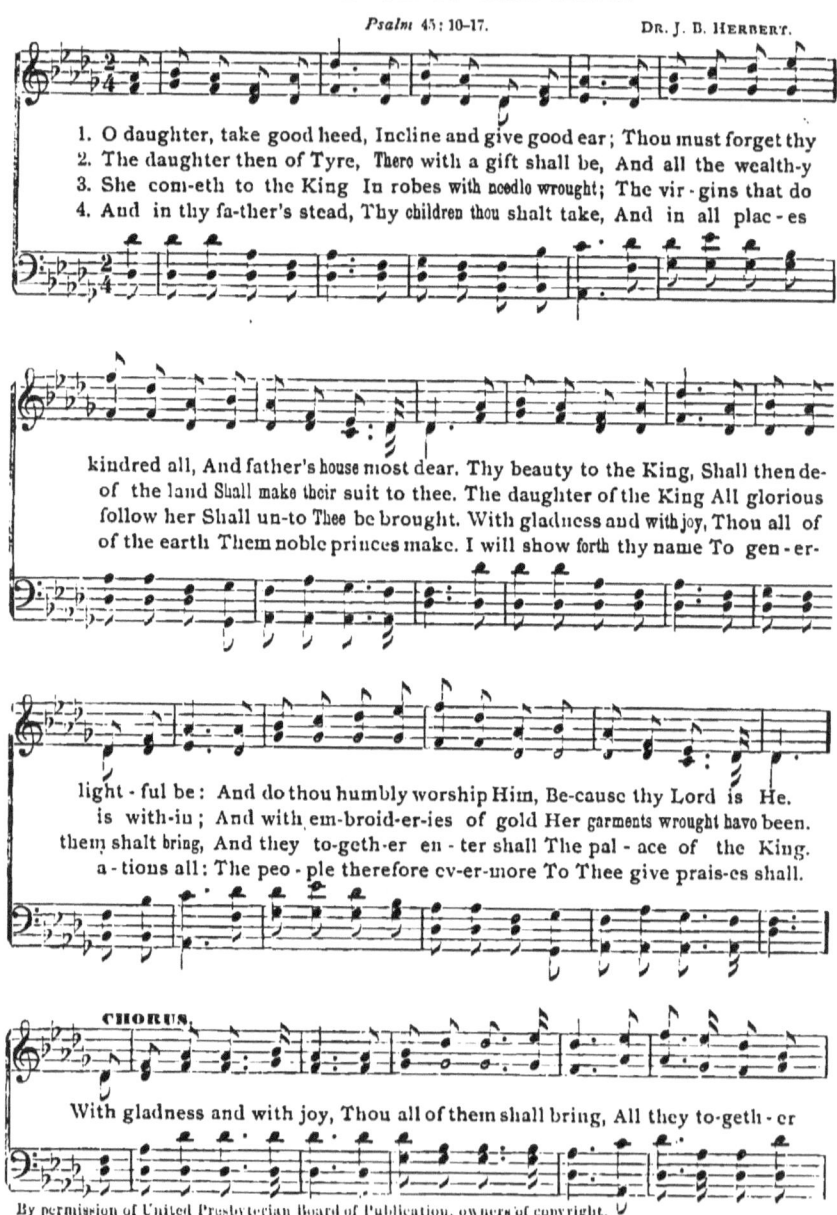

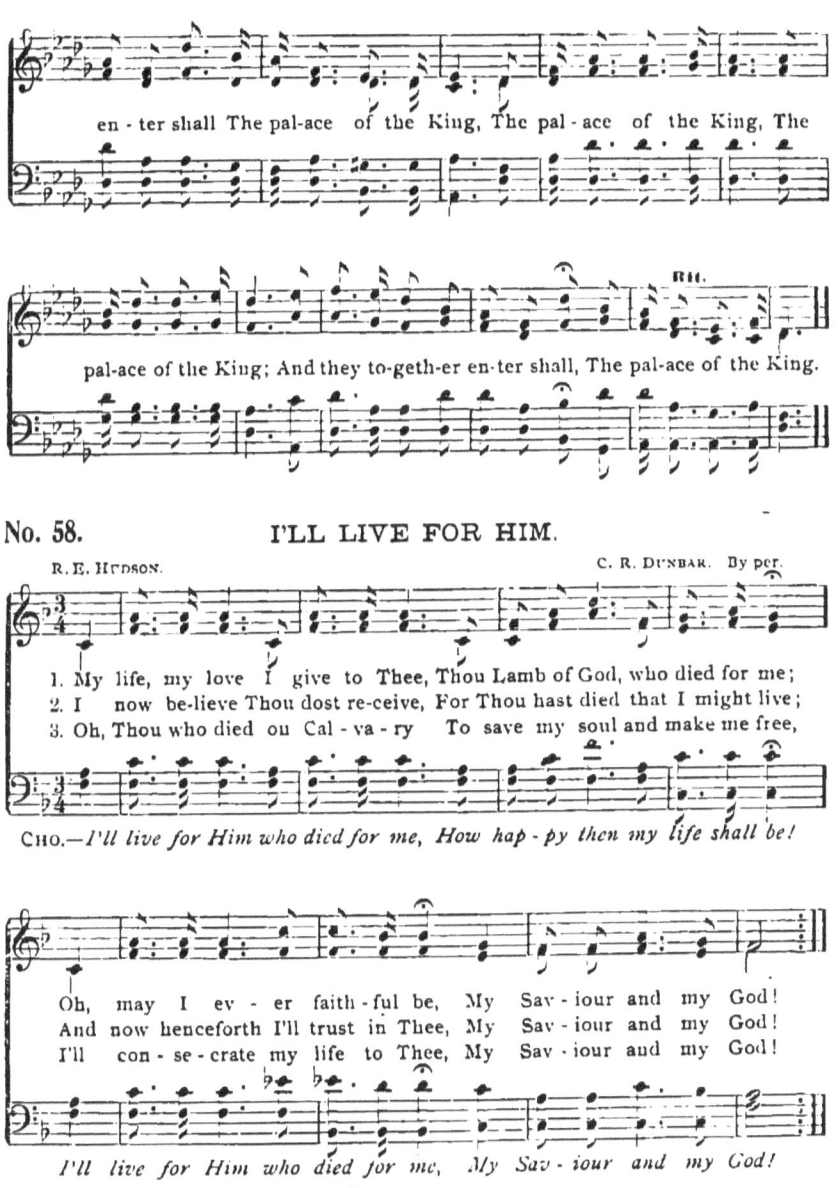

No. 59. THE HOME OVER THERE.

"*O that I had wings like a dove, for then would I fly away and be at rest.*"

Rev. D. W. C. Huntington. Tullius C. O'Kane, by per.

THE HOME OVER THERE. Concluded.

there, o-ver there, o-ver there, o-ver there, Oh, think of the home o-ver there.
there, o-ver there, o-ver there, o-ver there, Oh, think of the friends o-ver there.
there, o-ver there, o-ver there, o-ver there, My Sav-iour is now o-ver there.
there, o-ver there, o-ver there, o-ver there, I'll soon be at home o-ver there.

o - ver there,

No. 60.   THERE IS A FOUNTAIN.
WM. COWPER.   WESTERN MELODY. C. M.

1. There is a foun-tain filled with blood, Drawn from Im-man-uel's veins;
2. The dy-ing thief re-joiced to see That foun-tain in his day;
3. Ere since, by faith, I saw the stream Thy flow-ing wounds sup-ply,
4. Then in a no-bler, sweet-er song, I'll sing Thy power to save,

FINE.

And sin-ners plunged be-neath that flood, Lose all their guilt-y stains,
And there may I, though vile as he, Wash all my sins a way,
Re-deem-ing love has been my theme, And shall be till I die,
When this poor, lisp-ing, stam-m'ring tongue Lies si-lent in the grave,

D. S.

Lose all their guilt-y stains, . . Lose all their guilt-y stains,
Wash all my sins a-way, . . Wash all my sins a-way,
And shall be t l I die, . . . And shall be till I die,
Lies si-lent in the grave, . . Lies si-lent in the grave,

No. 63. GO WORK IN MY VINEYARD.

"Go work to-day in my vineyard."

ANON. From "Dew-drops," by per. of T. C. O'KANE.

1. "Go work in My vine-yard," "There's plenty to do, The har-vest is great and the la-b'rers are few; There's weeding and fenc-ing, and clear-ing of roots, And plough-ing and sow-ing, and gath'ring the fruits. There are fox-es to take, there are wolves to de-stroy, All a-ges and ranks I can ful-ly em-ploy. Go

2. "Go work in My vine-yard," "I claim thee as Mine. With blood did I buy thee, and all that is thine; I've sheep to be tend-ed, and lambs to be fed, The warm-est af-fec-tions, thy sun-ni-est hours, I wil-ling-ly yield-ed My king-dom for thee, The song of arch-an-gels—to hang on the tree;

D.S. *Thy time and thy tal-ents, thy loft-i-est powers, Thy paid thy full ran-som; My pur-chase I claim. (Go to Chorus.)*

D.S. *In pain and temp-ta-tion, in an-guish and shame, I lost must be gath-ered, the wea-ry ones led. (Go to Chorus.)*

GO WORK IN MY VINEYARD. Concluded.

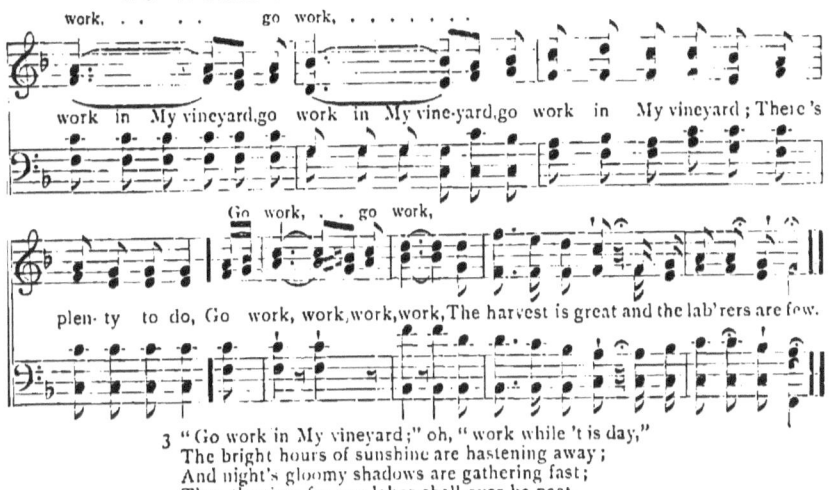

3 "Go work in My vineyard;" oh, "work while 't is day,"
The bright hours of sunshine are hastening away;
And night's gloomy shadows are gathering fast;
Then the time for our labor shall ever be past.
Begin in the morning, and toil all the day,
Thy strength I'll supply and thy wages I'll pay;
And blessed, thrice blessed the diligent few,
Who finish the labor I've given them to do.

No. 64. I STRETCH MY HANDS TO THEE.
CHARLES WESLEY. Tune: I DO BELIEVE. C.M.

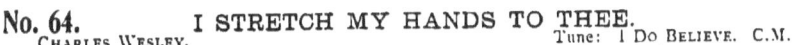

1. Father! I stretch my hands to Thee, No other help I know;
2. What did Thine only Son endure, Be-fore I drew my breath;
3. O Jesus, could I this believe, I now should feel Thy power;
4. Author of faith, to Thee I lift My weary, longing eyes;
CHO. I do believe I now believe, That Jesus died for me,

If Thou withdraw Thyself from me, Ah, whither shall I go?
What pain, what labor to secure My soul from endless death!
And all my wants thou wouldst relieve, In this accepted hour.
Oh let me now receive that gift! My soul without it dies.
And thro' His blood, His precious blood, I shall from sin be free.

No. 65. SCATTER SEEDS OF KINDNESS.

Mrs. Albert Smith. *"Be kindly affectioned one to another."* S. J. Vail, by per.

1. Let us gath-er up the sun-beams, Ly-ing all a-round our path; Let us keep the wheat and ro-ses, Cast-ing out the thorns and chaff, Let us find our sweetest com-fort In the bless-ings of to-day, With a pa-tient hand re-mov-ing All the bri-ars from the way. Then scat-ter seeds of kind-ness, Then scat-ter seeds of kind-ness, Then scat-ter seeds of kind-ness, For our reap-ing by and by.

2. Strange we nev-er prize the mu-sic Till the sweet-voiced bird is flown! Strange that we should slight the vio-lets Till the lovely flowers are gone! Strange that summer skies and sunshine Nev-er seem one half so fair, As when win-ter's snowy pinions Shake the white down in the air.

3. If we knew the ba-by fin-gers, Pressed against the win-dow pane, Would be cold and stiff to-morrow—Nev-er trou-ble us a-gain—Would the bright eyes of our dar-ling Catch the frown up-on our brow?—Would the prints of rosy fin-gers Vex us then as they do now.

4. Ah! those lit-tle ice-cold fin-gers, How they point our memories back To the has-ty words and ac-tions Strewn along our backward track! How those little hand re-mind us, As in snow-y grace they lie, Not to scat-ter thorns—but roses—For our reap-ing by and by.

By permission of Biglow & Main Co.

No. 67.   HIS YOKE IS EASY.

R. E. HUDSON. By per.

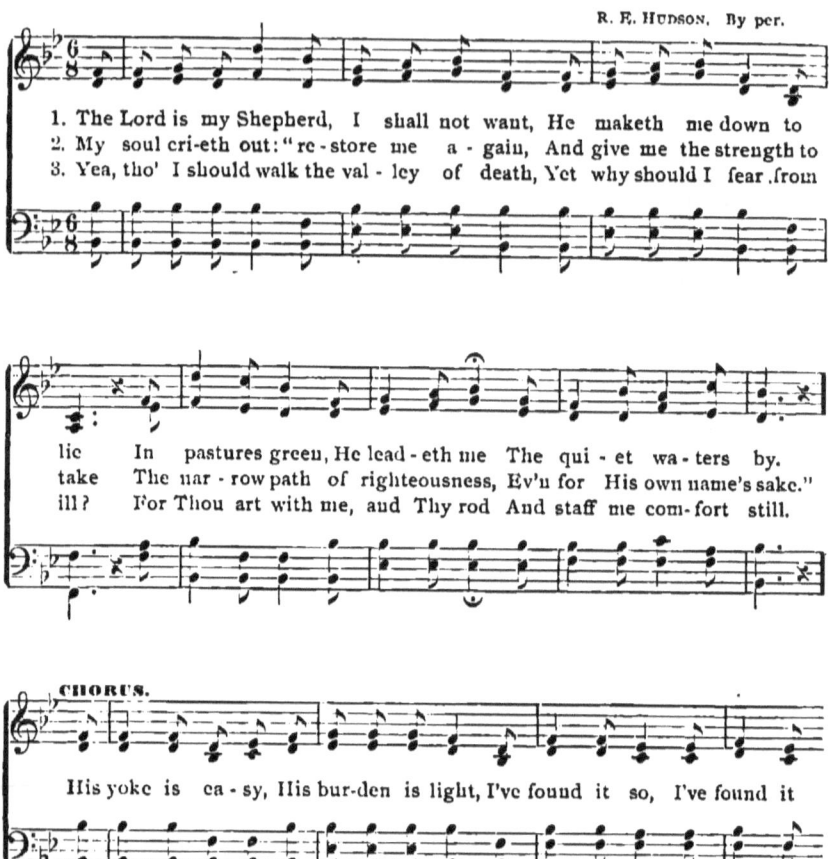

No. 70. GATHER AT THE RIVER.

ROBERT LOWRY, by per.

1. Shall we gath-er at the riv - er, Where bright an - gel feet have trod,
2. On the mar-gin of the riv - er, Dash - ing up its sil - ver spray,
3. Ere we reach the shin-ing riv - er, Lay we ev - 'ry bur - den down;
4. Soon we'll reach that sil - ver riv - er, Soon our pil-grimage shall cease;

With its crys - tal tide for ev - er, Flow-ing by the throne of God?
We will walk and wor - ship ev - er, All the hap - py, gold - en day.
Grace our spir - its will de - liv - er, And pro-vide a robe and crown.
Soon our hap - py hearts will quiv - er With the mel - o - dy of peace.

CHORUS. *p*

Yes, we'll gath-er at the riv - er, The beau - ti - ful, the beau - ti - ful riv - er—

Gath - er with the saints at the riv - er That flows by the throne of God.

No. 72. NEARER THE CROSS.

"*The cross of our Lord Jesus Christ.*"

F. J. CROSBY. Mrs. J. F. KNAPP, by per.

No. 76. IN THE ROYAL ARMY.

FANNY J. CROSBY. W. H. DOANE.

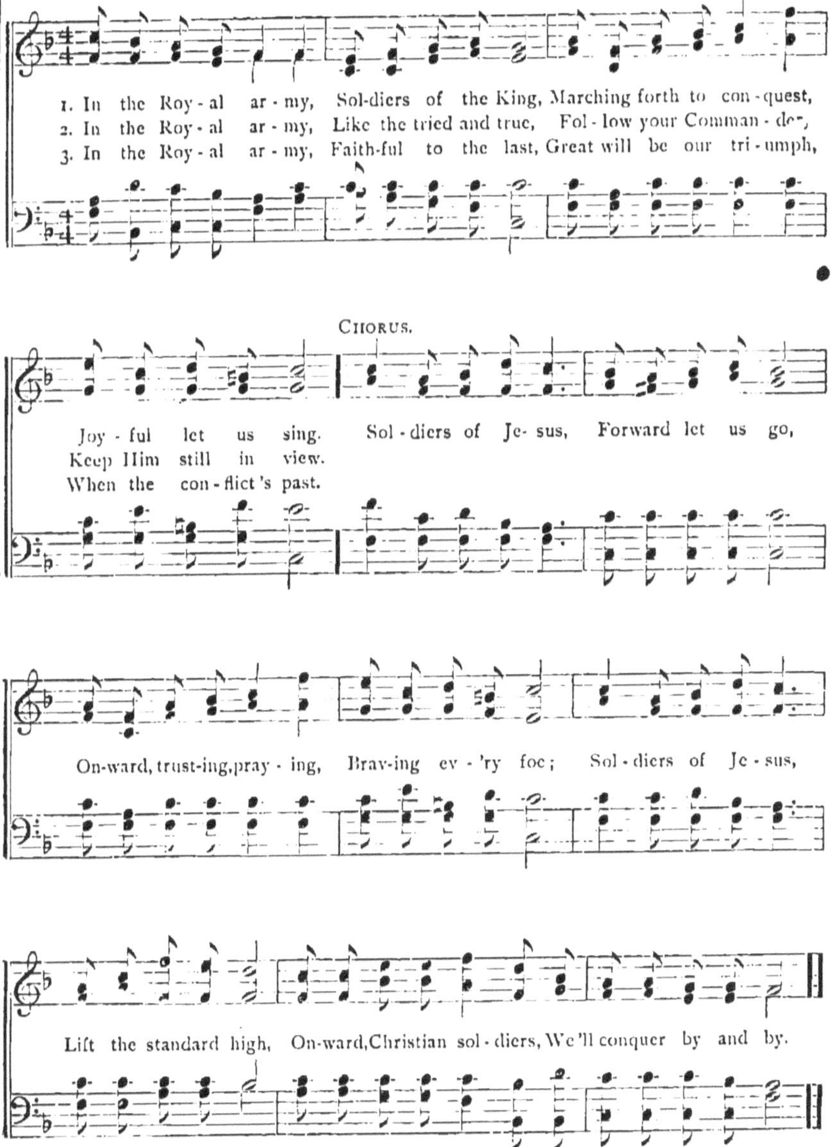

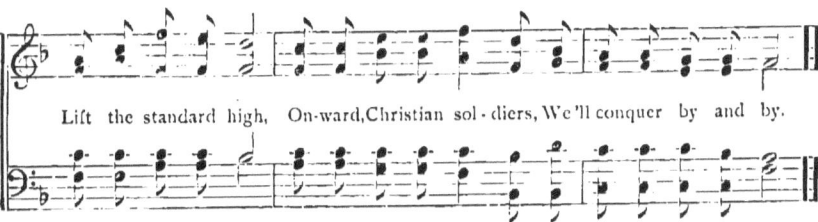

JOY IN HEAVEN. Concluded.

Souls are seek-ing now the liv-ing way; There is joy, joy, joy, joy a-mong the an-gels; Join their hal-le-lu-jah songs to-day. (to-day.)

No. 80. THERE'S A WIDENESS IN GOD'S MERCY.

FREDERICK W. FABER.   *Ps.* 136: 1-25.   LIZZIE S. TOURJEE. By per.

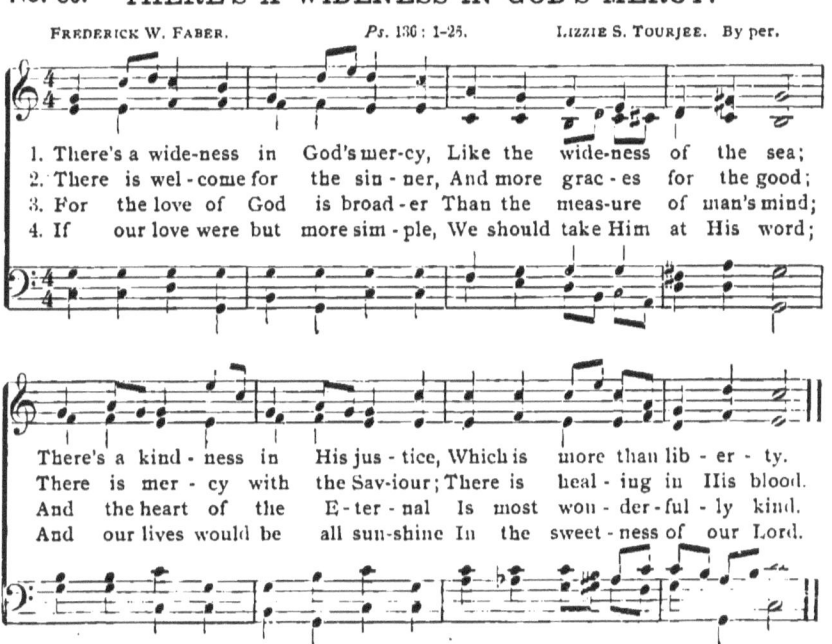

1. There's a wide-ness in God's mer-cy, Like the wide-ness of the sea;
2. There is wel-come for the sin-ner, And more grac-es for the good;
3. For the love of God is broad-er Than the meas-ure of man's mind;
4. If our love were but more sim-ple, We should take Him at His word;

There's a kind-ness in His jus-tice, Which is more than lib-er-ty.
There is mer-cy with the Sav-iour; There is heal-ing in His blood.
And the heart of the E-ter-nal Is most won-der-ful-ly kind.
And our lives would be all sun-shine In the sweet-ness of our Lord.

HE SAVED ME. Concluded.

3 But there in that dark lonely hour,
  Came a voice sweetly whispering to me,
  Saying Christ, the Redeemer, hath power
  ‖: To save a poor sinner like me.:‖

4 I listened, and lo! 'twas the Saviour,
  Then speaking so kindly to me;
  And now unto others I'm telling,
  ‖: How He saved a poor sinner like me.:‖

5 I then fully trusted in Jesus,
  And oh, what a joy came to me;
  My heart it was filled with His praises,
  ‖: For saving a sinner like me.:‖

6 And when this life's journey is over,
  And I the dear Saviour shall see;
  I'll praise Him forever and ever,
  ‖: For saving a sinner like me.:‖

No. 82. CHEER THEE, SAD SOUL.

"*Be of good cheer.*"   Dr. Thos. Hastings.

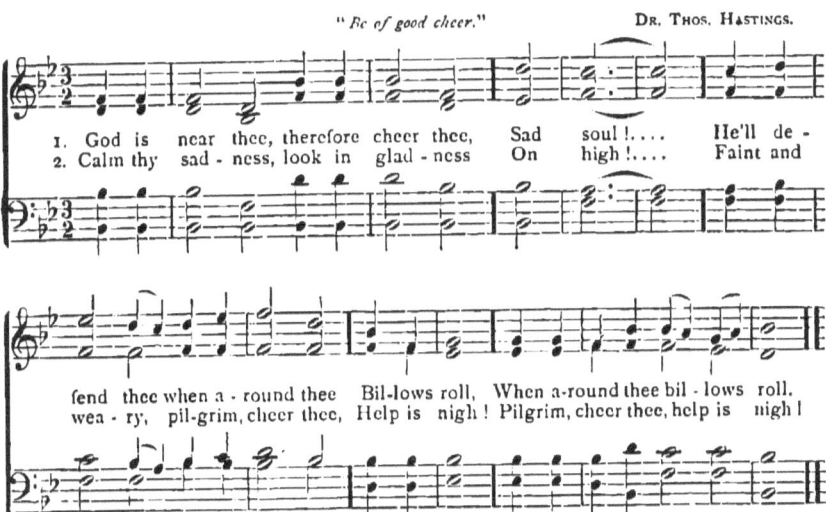

3 Mark the sea-bird wildly wheeling
    Through the skies!
  God defends him, God attends him
    When he cries!
  God attends him when he cries.

4 God is near thee, therefore cheer thee,
    Sad soul!
  He'll defend thee, when around thee
    Billows roll!
  When around thee billows roll.

2 "Almost persuaded," come, come to-day ;
"Almost persuaded," turn not away ;
Jesus invites you here,
Angels are ling'ring near,
Prayers rise from hearts so dear :
O wanderer, come !

3 "Almost persuaded," harvest is past ;
"Almost persuaded," doom comes at last ;
Almost cannot avail,
Almost is but to fail ;
Sad, sad that better wail—
Almost—but lost.

No. 85. JESUS OF NAZARETH.
Miss EMMA CAMPBELL.   T. E. PERKINS. By per.

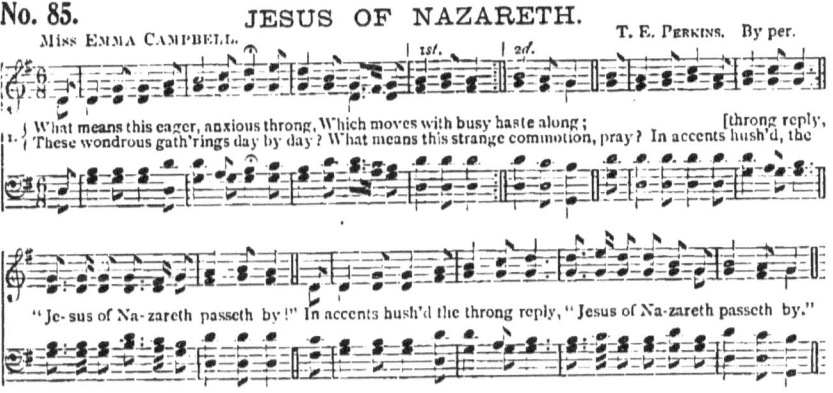

2 Who is this Jesus? Why should He
The city move so mightily?
A passing stranger, has he skill
To move the multitude at will?
|: Again the stirring tones reply,
" Jesus of Nazareth passeth by." :|

3 Jesus! 'tis He who once below
Man's pathway trod 'mid pain and woe ;
And burdened ones, where'er He came,
Brought out their sick, and deaf, and lame ;
|: The blind rejoice to hear the cry :
" Jesus of Nazareth passeth by." :|

4 Ho! all ye heavy-laden, come ;
Here's pardon, comfort, rest, and home.
Ye wanderers from a Father's face,
Return, accept His proffered grace.
|: Ye tempted ones, there's refuge nigh :
" Jesus of Nazareth passeth by." :|

5 But if you still this call refuse,
And all His wondrous love abuse,
Soon will He sadly from you turn,
Your bitter prayer for pardon spurn.
|: "Too late! too late !" will be the cry :
" Jesus of Nazareth *has passed by*." :|

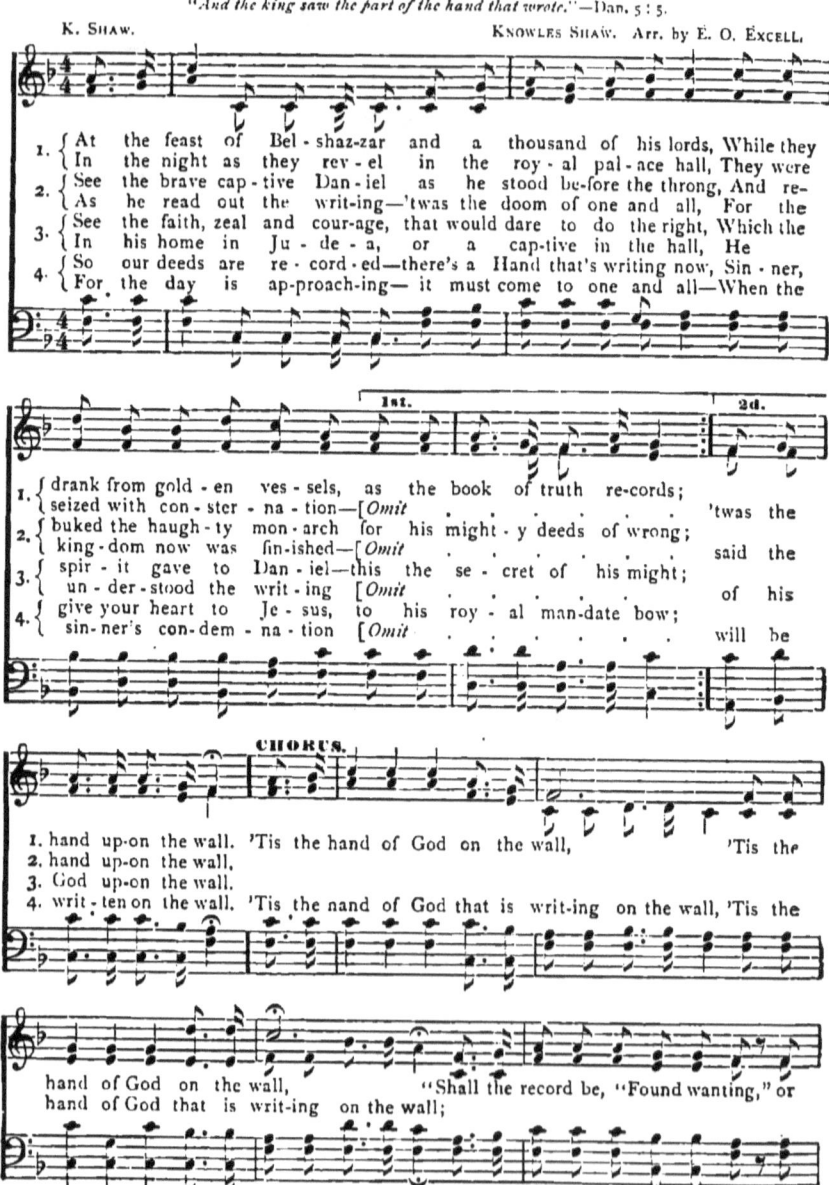

THE HANDWRITING ON THE WALL. Concluded.

shall it be, "Found trusting?" While that hand is writing on the wall,
writ-ing on the wall.

No. 87.   NEARER TO ME.

E. A. Hoffman.   William A. Galfin, by per.

1. Draw near, O Christ! to me, Near-er to me, Un-worth-y and un-
2. Draw near, O Christ! to me, Near-er to me, My soul with strong de-
3. Draw near, O Christ! to me, Near-er to me, Let all thy wealth of

clean Though I may be; Come with thy quick-'ning grace, Show me thy
sire Burns af-ter thee; Let me thy joys par-take, Come, ere my
love Fall up-on me; Touch ev-'ry se-cret sin, Wash me and

smil-ing face, Draw near this hal-lowed place, Draw near to me.
spir-it break, For thy sweet mer-cy's sake, Draw near to me.
make me clean, Let noth-ing stand be-tween My heart and thee.

No. 88. LIFE'S HARVEST

"The harvest truly is plenteous, but the laborers are few."

Spirited. I. B. WOODBURY. By per.

1. Ho! reap-ers of life's har-vest, Why stand with rusted blade, Un-til the night draws round thee,
D. S. The gold-en morn is pass-ing,
And day be-gins to fade? Why stand ye i-dle, wait-ing For reap-ers more to come?
Why sit ye i-dle, dumb?

2 Thrust in your sharpened sickle,
 And gather in the grain,
The night is fast approaching,
 And soon will come again.
The Master calls for reapers,
 And shall He call in vain?
Shall sheaves lie there ungathered,
 And waste upon the plain?

3 Mount up the heights of Wisdom,
 And crush each error low;
Keep back no words of knowledge
 That human hearts should know.
Be faithful to thy mission,
 In service of thy Lord,
And then a golden chaplet
 Shall be thy just reward.

No. 89. CHRISTIAN'S MISSION.

T. C. O'KANE.

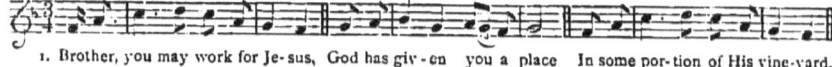

1. Brother, you may work for Je-sus, God has giv-en you a place In some por-tion of His vine-yard,

And will give sus-tain-ing grace. He has bid-den you "Go la-bor," And has promised a re-ward;

rit.

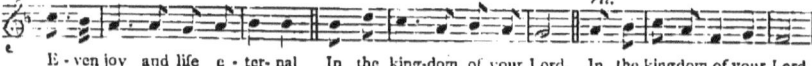

E-ven joy and life e-ter-nal In the king-dom of your Lord, In the kingdom of your Lord.

2 Brother, you may pray to Jesus
 In your closet and at home;
In the village, in the city,
 Or wherever you may roam.
Pray that God may send the Spirit
 Into some dear sinner's heart,
And that in his soul's salvation
 ‖: You may bear some humble part. :‖

3 Sister, you may "sing for Jesus,"
 O, how precious is His love!
Praise Him for His boundless blessings
 Ever coming from above.

Sing how Jesus died to save you,
 How your sins and guilt He bore;
How His blood hath sealed your pardon;
 ‖: "Sing for Jesus" evermore. :‖

4 Brother, you may live for Jesus,
 Him who died that you may live;
O, then all your ransomed powers
 Cheerful to His service give.
Thus for Jesus you may labor,
 And for Jesus sing and pray;
Consecrate your life to Jesus;
 ‖: Love and serve Him every day. :‖

No. 90. BRINGING IN THE SHEAVES!

"*He that goeth forth and weepeth, bearing precious seed, shall doubtless come again with rejoicing, bringing his sheaves with him.*"

KNOWLES SHAW.
Arr. from G. A. MINER.

1. Sow-ing in the morn-ing, sow-ing seeds of kindness, Sow-ing in the noon-tide and the dew-y eves; Wait-ing for the har-vest, and the time of reap-ing,

REFRAIN.

We shall come re-joic-ing, bringing in the sheaves! Bringing in the sheaves! bringing in the sheaves! We shall come re-joic-ing, bringing in the sheaves! bringing in the sheaves!

1st time. *2d time.* *Repeat pp*

2 Sowing in the sunshine, sowing in the shadows,
  Fearing neither clouds nor winter's chilling breeze:
  By and by the harvest, and the labor ended,
  We shall come rejoicing, bringing in the sheaves!

3 Go, then, ever weeping, sowing for the Master,
  Though the loss sustained our spirit often grieves:
  When our weeping's over, He will bid us welcome,
  We shall come rejoicing, bringing in the sheaves!

2 God be with you till we meet again,
  'Neath his wings securely hide you;
  Daily manna still divide you,
God be with you till we meet again.—Cho.

3 God be with you till we meet again,
  When life's perils thick confound you;
  Put his arms unfailing round you,
God be with you till we meet again.—Cho.

4 God be with you till me meet again,
  Keep love's banner floating o'er you;
  Smite death's threatening wave before you,
God be with you till we meet again.—Cho.

Rev. J. E. Rankin.

3 A sweet perfume upon the breeze
  Is borne from ever vernal trees;
  And flow'rs that never fading grow
  Where streams of life forever flow.—*Cho.*

4 The zephyrs seem to float to me
  Sweet sounds of heav'ns melody,
  As angels, with the white-rob'd throng,
  Join in the sweet redemption song.—*Cho.*

No. 93. LET THE CHILDREN COME.
PHILIP PHILLIPS.

1. In the early spring-time, When your leaves are fair, Little buds of promise, Little blossoms rare;
2. All the lit-tle chil-dren Gladly will we bring To the arms of Jesus, Heav'n's exalt-ed King;

Hear the words of Je-sus, Precious will they be, Bring the lit-tle chil-dren, Let them come to Me.
For the in - vi - ta - tion, Gracious, full, and free, Says to *all* the children, Let them come to Me.

CHORUS.
Let them come to Me, Let them come to Me, Bring the little children, Let them come to Me.

3 Let them come in welcome
  To My bleeding side,
To secure their pardon
  I was crucified :
They may be forgiven,
  From the law set free,
I, the Lord, have risen,
  Let them come to Me.—*Cho.*

4 Jesus, we are coming
  To Thy loving arms,
Safely there reposing,
  Sin no longer harms.
From the wiles of Satan
  Thou canst set us free,
Though we're little children,
  We will come to Thee.—*Cho.*

No. 94. BEAUTIFUL, THE LITTLE HANDS.
"*Something for each to do.*"
BISHOP W. JOHNS.

1. Beau-ti- ful the little hands, That ful-fill the Lord's commands; Beauti-ful the little eyes,

CHORUS.
Kindled with light from the skies. Beautiful, beautiful, lit-tle hands, That ful- fill the

From " Gospel Bells," By permission of H. A. Sumner & Co., Chicago.

BEAUTIFUL, THE LITTLE HANDS. Concluded.

2 All the little hands were made
Jesus' precious cause to aid;
All the little hearts to beat
Warm in his service so sweet.
CHO.—Beautiful, &c.

3 All the little lips should pray
To the Saviour, every day;

All the little feet should go
Swift on his errands below,
CHO.—Beautiful, &c.

3 What your little hands can do,
That the Lord intends for you;
Make that thing your first delight,
Do it to him with your might.
CHO.—Beautiful, &c.

T. CORBEN.

No. 95.   WHEN THE KING COMES IN.

"The Wedding Garment."   E. S. LORENZ.

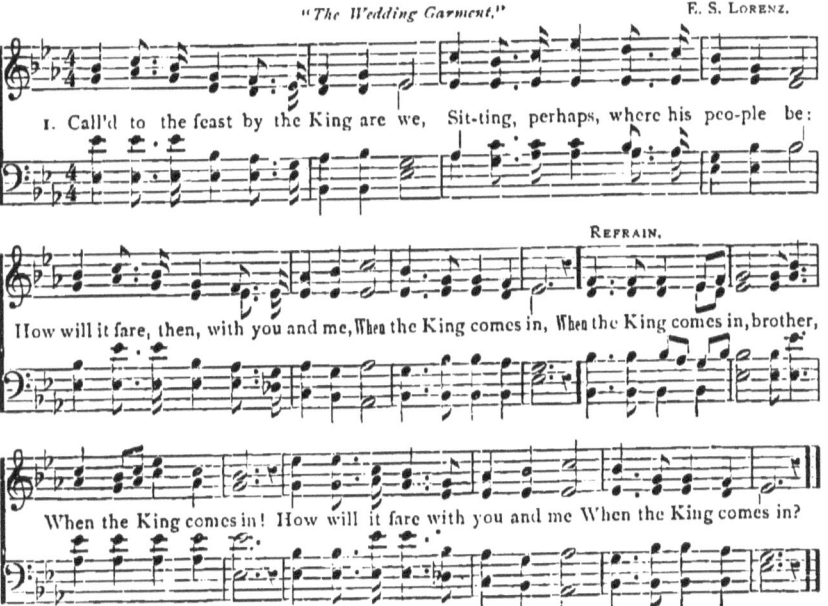

From "Songs of Grace," by per.

2 Crowns on the head where the thorns have [been,
Glorified he who once died for men;
Splendid the vision before us then,
When the King comes in.—REF.

3 Like lightning's flash will that instant show
Things hidden long from both friend and foe,

Just what we are, every one will know,
When the King comes in.—REF.

4 Joyful his eyes on each one shall rest
Who is in white wedding garments dressed—
Ah! well for us if we stand the test,
When the King comes in.—REF.

J. E. LANDOR.

No. 96. LEAD, KINDLY LIGHT.

J. B. Dykes.

1. Lead, kind-ly Light, a-mid th'en-circling gloom, Lead Thou me on; The night is dark, and I am far from home, Lead Thou me on.... Keep Thou my feet; I do not ask to see...... The dis-tant scene; one step e-nough for me. A-men.

2.
I was not ever thus, nor prayed that Thou
    Shouldst lead me on;
I loved to choose and see my path; but now
    Lead Thou me on.
I loved the garish day; and spite of fears,
Pride ruled my will: remember not past
    years.

3.
So long Thy power has blest me, sure it still
    Will lead me on
O'er moor and fen, o'er crag and torrent, till
    The night is gone,
And with the morn those angel faces smile,
Which I have loved long since, and lost
    awhile. Amen.
        John H. Newman.

No. 97. NOTHING BUT THE BLOOD OF JESUS.

"Without shedding of blood is no remission."

Copyright, 1876. Words and Music by Rev. ROBERT LOWRY.

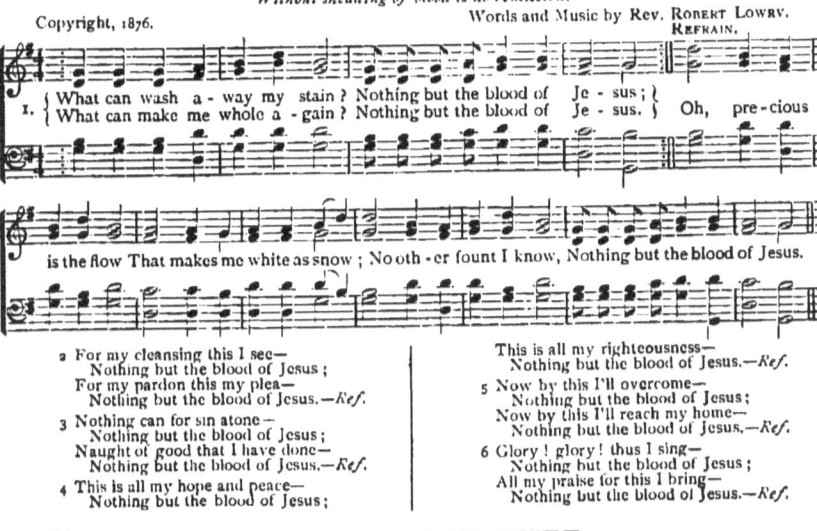

2 For my cleansing this I see—
  Nothing but the blood of Jesus;
  For my pardon this my plea—
  Nothing but the blood of Jesus.—*Ref.*

3 Nothing can for sin atone—
  Nothing but the blood of Jesus;
  Naught of good that I have done—
  Nothing but the blood of Jesus.—*Ref.*

4 This is all my hope and peace—
  Nothing but the blood of Jesus;

This is all my righteousness—
  Nothing but the blood of Jesus.—*Ref.*

5 Now by this I'll overcome—
  Nothing but the blood of Jesus;
  Now by this I'll reach my home—
  Nothing but the blood of Jesus.—*Ref.*

6 Glory! glory! thus I sing—
  Nothing but the blood of Jesus;
  All my praise for this I bring—
  Nothing but the blood of Jesus.—*Ref.*

No. 98. THIS I DID FOR THEE.

"He was bruised for our iniquities."   PHILIP PHILLIPS.

2 I spent long years for thee,
  In weariness and woe,
  That one eternity
  Of joy thou mightest know.
  I spent long years for thee, for thee;
  |: Hast thou spent *one* for Me, for Me? :|

3 And I have brought to thee,
  Down from My house above,
  Salvation full and free,

My pardon and My love.
  Great gifts I brought to thee, to thee;
  |: What hast thou *brought* to Me, to Me? :|

4 Oh, let thy life be given,
  Thy years for Me be spent,
  World fetters all be riven,
  And joy with suffering blent.
  Give thou *thyself* to Me, to Me,
  |: And I will welcome thee, *yes*, thee! :|

No. 100. ART THOU WEARY? 8,5,8,3.
"This is the rest wherewith ye may cause the weary to rest."

H. W. Baker, Bart.

1 Art thou weary, art thou languid,
   Art thou sore distrest?
   "Come to me," saith One, " and coming
   Be at rest!"
2 Hath He marks to lead me to Him,
   If He be my guide?
   "In His feet and hands are wound-prints,
   And His side."
3 Hath He diadem as monarch
   That His brow adorns?
   "Yea, a crown, in very surety,
   But of thorns!"

4 If I find Him, if I follow,
   What His guerdon here?
   "Many a sorrow, many a labor,
   Many a tear."
5 If I still hold closely to Him,
   What hath He at last?
   "Sorrow vanquished, labor ended,
   Jordan past."
6 If I ask Him to receive me,
   Will He say me nay?
   "Not till earth, and not till heaven
   Pass away."

No. 101. CONSECRATION HYMN.
"Neither count I my life dear unto myself."

F. R. Havergal. From Mozart.

3 Take my voice, and let me sing
   Always, only, for my King;
   Take my lips, and let them be
   Filled with messages from Thee.
4 Take my silver and my gold;
   Not a mite would I withhold;
   Take my intellect, and use
   Every power as thou shalt choose.

5 Take my will, and make it Thine;
   It shall be no longer mine;
   Take my heart; it is Thine own,
   It shall be Thy royal throne.
6 Take my love; my Lord, I pour
   At Thy feet its treasure-store;
   Take myself, and I will be
   Ever, only, ALL for Thee.

No. 102. EVENING SHADES. 8s & 7s.

D. A. Jones.

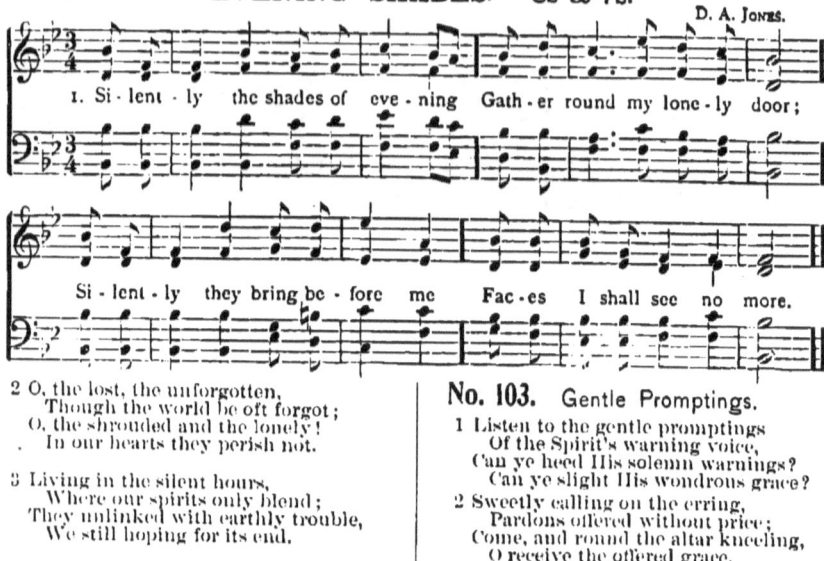

1. Si-lent-ly the shades of eve-ning Gath-er round my lone-ly door;
Si-lent-ly they bring be-fore me Fac-es I shall see no more.

2 O, the lost, the unforgotten,
   Though the world be oft forgot;
O, the shrouded and the lonely!
   In our hearts they perish not.

3 Living in the silent hours,
   Where our spirits only blend;
They unlinked with earthly trouble,
   We still hoping for its end.

4 How such holy mem'ries cluster,
   Like the stars when storms are past,
Pointing up to that fair haven
   We may hope to gain at last.

No. 103. Gentle Promptings.

1 Listen to the gentle promptings
   Of the Spirit's warning voice,
Can ye heed His solemn warnings?
   Can ye slight His wondrous grace?

2 Sweetly calling on the erring,
   Pardons offered without price;
Come, and round the altar kneeling,
   O receive the offered grace.

3 Joy and hope the troubled conscience
   Will allay with soothing peace;
Press we then to realms of glory,
   Run with joy the heavenly race.

No. 104. ROCK OF AGES. 7s, 6 lines.

"*But the Lord is my defence, and my God is the rock of my refuge.*" Dr. T. Hastings.

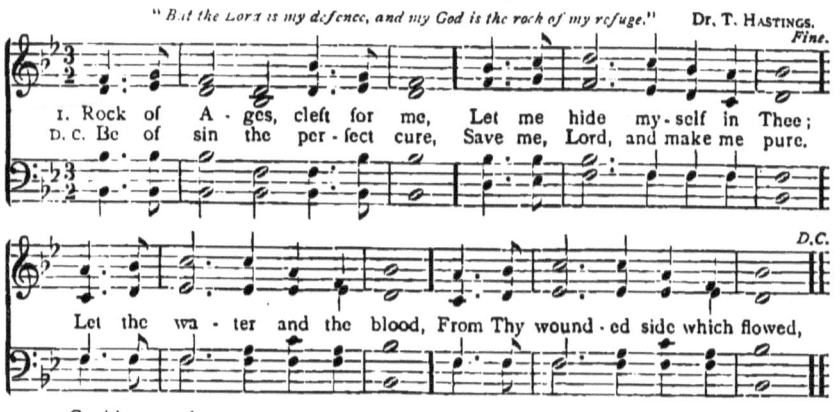

1. Rock of A-ges, cleft for me, Let me hide my-self in Thee;
D.C. Be of sin the per-fect cure, Save me, Lord, and make me pure.
Let the wa-ter and the blood, From Thy wound-ed side which flowed,

2 Could my zeal no respite know,
   Could my tears forever flow,
   This for sin could ne'er atone,
   Thou must save, and Thou alone;
   In my hand no price I bring,
   Simply to Thy cross I cling.

3 While I draw this fleeting breath,
   When mine eyelids close in death,
   When I soar to worlds unknown,
   And behold Thee on Thy throne,
   Rock of Ages! cleft for me,
   Let me hide myself in Thee.—**Toplady.**

No. 105. HOME OF THE SOUL.

"And there shall in no wise enter into it anything that defileth, neither whatsoever worketh abomination or maketh a lie; but they which are written in the Lamb's Book of Life."

PHILIP PHILLIPS, from "Singing Pilgrim."

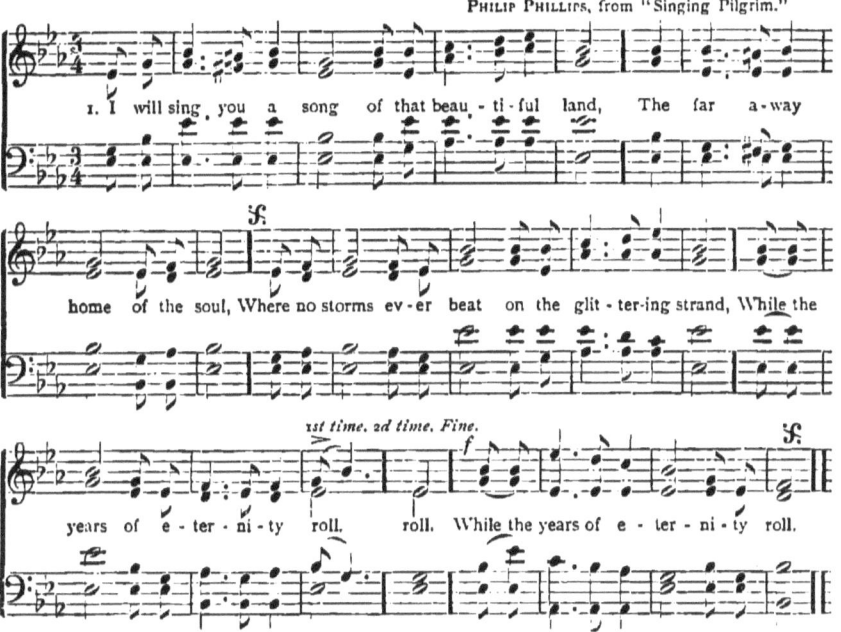

1. I will sing you a song of that beau-ti-ful land, The far a-way home of the soul, Where no storms ev-er beat on the glit-ter-ing strand, While the years of e-ter-ni-ty roll. roll. While the years of e-ter-ni-ty roll.

2 O that home of the soul in my visions and dreams,
Its bright jasper walls I can see,
Till I fancy but thinly the veil intervenes
‖: Between the fair city and me. :‖

3 There the great tree of life in its beauty doth grow,
And the river of life floweth by ;
For no death ever enters that city, you know,
‖: And nothing that maketh a lie ; :‖

4 That unchangeable home is for you and for me,
Where Jesus of Nazareth stands ;
The King of all kingdoms forever is He,
‖: And He holdeth our crowns in His hands. :‖

5 O how sweet it will be in that beautiful land,
So free from all sorrow and pain !
With songs on our lips and with harps in our hands,
‖: To meet one another again. :‖
Gates.

No. 106. THE GLORY LAND.
S. M.

1 FAR from these scenes of night,
Unbounded glories rise,
And realms of joy and pure delight
Unknown to mortal eyes.

2 Fair land !—could mortal eyes
But half its charms explore,
How would our spirits long to rise,
And dwell on earth no more !

3 No cloud those regions know,—
Realms ever bright and fair !
For sin, the source of mortal woe,
Can never enter there.

4 O may the prospect fire
Our hearts with ardent love,
Till wings of faith, and strong desire,
Bear every thought above. Steele.

No. 107. LOVE DIVINE. 8s & 7s.

"The chiefest among ten thousands."

Andante con moto. JOHN ZUNDEL.

1. Love di-vine, all love ex-celling, Joy of heav'n, to earth come down! Fix in us Thy humble dwelling,
D. S. Vis - it us with Thy sal - va-tion,

All Thy faithful mercies crown. Je-sus, Thou art all com-pas-sion, Pure, unbounded love Thou art;
En - ter every trembling heart.

2 Breathe, O breathe Thy loving spirit
Into every troubled breast!
Let us all in Thee inherit,
Let us find the promised rest.
Come, almighty to deliver,
Let us all Thy life receive!
Speedily return, and never,
Never more Thy temples leave!

3 Finish then Thy new creation,
Pure, unspotted may we be:
Let us see our whole salvation
Perfectly secured by Thee!
Changed from glory into glory,
Till in heaven we take our place;
Till we cast our crowns before Thee,
Lost in wonder, love, and praise.
CHARLES WESLEY.

No. 108. COME TO THE FOUNTAIN.

"Waiting to save."

GEO. C. STEBBINS.

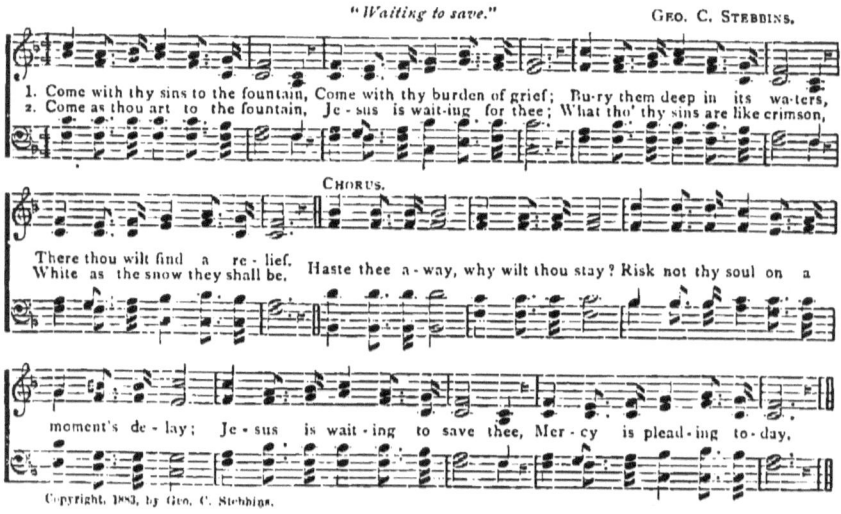

1. Come with thy sins to the fountain, Come with thy burden of grief; Bu-ry them deep in its wa-ters,
2. Come as thou art to the fountain, Je - sus is wait-ing for thee; What tho' thy sins are like crimson,

CHORUS.

There thou wilt find a re - lief.
White as the snow they shall be. Haste thee a - way, why wilt thou stay? Risk not thy soul on a

moment's de - lay; Je - sus is wait - ing to save thee, Mer - cy is plead - ing to - day.

Copyright, 1883, by Geo. C. Stebbins.

3 These are the words of the Saviour;
They who repent and believe,
They who are willing to trust Him,
Life at His hand shall receive.
Cho.—Haste thee away, etc.

4 Come and be healed at the fountain,
List to the peace-speaking voice;
Over a sinner returning
Now let the angels rejoice.
Cho.—Haste thee away, etc.
FANNY J. CROSBY.

No. 109. REDEEMED.

"Behold the Lamb of God, which taketh away the sin of the world!"

T. C.   T. C. O'KANE.

1. O, sing of Jesus, "Lamb of God," Who died on Calvary, And for a ransom shed His blood For you, and even me. I'm redeemed,.. I'm redeemed,.... Thro' the blood of the Lamb that was slain,....... I'm redeemed,.... I'm redeemed,.... Hallelujah to God and the Lamb!

2 O wondrous power of love divine!
So pure, so full, so free!
It reaches out to all mankind,
Embraces even me.
I'm redeemed, &c.

3 All glory now to Christ the Lord,
And evermore shall be!
He hath redeemed a world of sin,
And ransomed even me.
I'm redeemed, &c.

No. 110. I AM PRAYING FOR YOU.

S. O. MALLEY CLIFF. *"Evening, and morning, and at noon, will I pray."* IRA D. SANKEY. By per.

1. I have a Sav-iour, He's pleading in glo-ry, A dear lov-ing Sav-iour, tho' earth-friends be few; And now He is watch-ing in ten-der-ness o'er me, And

CHORUS.

O that my Sav-iour were your Sav-iour too! For you I am pray-ing, For you I am pray-ing, For you I am pray-ing, I'm pray-ing for you.

2 I have a Father; to me He has given
  A hope for eternity, blessed and true;
  And soon He will call me to meet Him in heaven;
  But O, may He lead you to go with me too!—*Cho.*

3 I have a robe; 'tis resplendent in whiteness,
  Awaiting in glory my wondering view;
  O, when I receive it all shining in brightness,
  Dear friend, could I see you receiving one too!—*Cho.*

4 I have a peace; it is calm as a river—
  A peace that the friends of this world never knew;
  My Saviour alone is its Author and Giver,
  And O, could I know it was given to you!—*Cho.*

5 When Jesus has found you, tell others the story,
  That my loving Saviour is your Saviour too;
  Then pray that your Saviour may bring them to glory,
  And prayer will be answered—'twas answered for you!—*Cho.*

No. III.   ETERNITY IS DRAWING NIGH.

"*The night is far spent, the day is at hand.*"

HORATIUS BONAR, D.D.   PHILIP PHILLIPS.

1. Pray, brethren, pray, The sands are fall-ing; Pray, brethren, pray, God's voice is call-ing; Yon tur-ret strikes the dy-ing chime, We kneel up-on the edge of time.
2. Praise, brethren, praise, The skies are rend-ing; Praise, brethren, praise, The fight is end-ing; Be-hold! the glo-ry draw-eth near, The King Him-self will soon ap-pear.

REFRAIN.
E-ter-ni-ty is draw-ing nigh, E-ter-ni-ty, E-ter-ni-ty, E-ter-ni-ty is draw-ing nigh.

3 Watch, brethren, watch,
  The day is dying;
Watch, brethren, watch,
  The time is flying;
Watch as men watch the starting breath,
Watch as men watch for life and death.

4 Look, brethren, look,
  The day is breaking;
Hark, brethren, hark,
  The dead are waking.
With girded loins all ready stand—
Behold! the Bridegroom is at hand.

* The next four measures sung in unison are very effective.

No. 114. MY CROSS I'VE TAKEN.

Henry F. Lyte. *"Take up thy cross and follow me."* Spanish.

1. Je-sus, I my cross have tak-en, All to leave and follow Thee; Naked, poor, despised, forsaken, Yet how rich is my con-di-tion, Thou from hence my all shalt be! Perish ev-'ry fond am-bi-tion, All I've sought, or hoped, or known; God and heav'n are still my own.

2 Let the world despise and leave me,
   They have left my Saviour, too;
   Human hearts and looks deceive me—
   Thou art not, like them, untrue;
   O! while Thou dost smile upon me,
   God of wisdom, love, and might,
   Foes may hate, and friends disown me,
   Show Thy face, and all is bright.

3 Haste thee on from grace to glory,
   Armed by faith, and winged by prayer!
   Heaven's eternal day's before thee;
   God's own hand will guide thee there;
   Soon shall close thy earthly mission,
   Soon shall pass thy pilgrim days,
   Hope shall change to glad fruition,
   Faith to sight, and prayer to praise.

No. 115. JESUS IS MINE.

H. Bonar. *"My Beloved is mine."* T. E. Perkins. By per.

1. Fade, fade each earthly joy, Je-sus is mine! Break ev-'ry ten-der tie, Je-sus is mine! Dark is the wild-erness, Earth has no resting-place, Je-sus a-lone can bless, Je-sus is mine!

2 Tempt not my soul away,
   Jesus is mine!
   Here would I ever stay,
   Jesus is mine!
   Perishing things of clay,
   Born but for one brief day,
   Pass from my heart away,
   Jesus is mine!

3 Farewell, ye dreams of night,
   Jesus is mine!
   Lost in this dawning light,
   Jesus is mine!

All that my soul has tried,
Left but a dismal void,
Jesus has satisfied,
Jesus is mine!

4 Farewell, mortality,
   Jesus is mine!
   Welcome, eternity,
   Jesus is mine!
   Welcome, O loved and blest,
   Welcome, sweet scenes of rest,
   Welcome, my Saviour's breast,
   Jesus is mine!

No. 116. WHILE THE YEARS ARE ROLLING ON.

Harriet B. McKeever. Jno. R. Sweney. By per.

1. In a world so full of weeping, While the years are rolling on, Christian souls the watch are keeping, While the years are rolling on. While our journey we pursue, With the haven still in view, There is work for us to do, While the years are rolling on.

CHORUS.
Are rolling on, are rolling on, Are rolling on, are rolling on, O, the good we may be doing, While the years are rolling on.

2 There's no time to waste in sighing,
  While the years are rolling on;
  Time is flying, souls are dying.
  While the years are rolling on.
  Loving words a soul may win
  From the wretched paths of sin;
  We may bring the wand'rers in,
  While the years are rolling on.—*Cho.*

3 Let us strengthen one another,
  While the years are rolling on;
  Seek to raise a fallen brother,
  While the years are rolling on.

  This is work for every hand,
  Till, throughout creation's land,
  Armies for the Lord shall stand,
  While the years are rolling on.—*Cho.*

4 Friends we love are quickly flying,
  While the years are rolling on;
  No more parting, no more dying,
  While the years are rolling on.
  In the world beyond the tomb
  Sorrow never more can come,
  When we meet in that blest home,
  While the years are rolling on.—*Cho.*

No. 117. A LITTLE TALK WITH JESUS.

FISCHER. By per.

1. A lit-tle talk with Je-sus, how it soothes the rug-ged road!
   How it seems to help me on-ward, when I faint be-neath my load!
   When my heart is crush'd with sor-row, and my eyes with tears are dim,
   There is nought can yield me com-fort like a lit-tle talk with Him.

2 I tell Him I am weary, and fain would be at rest;
  That I am daily, hourly longing to repose upon His breast;
  And He answers me so sweetly, in the tenderest tones of love,
  "I am coming soon to take thee to My happy home above."

3 The way is long and weary to yonder far-off clime,
  But a little talk with Jesus doth while away the time;
  The more I come to know Him, and all His grace explore,
  It sets me ever longing to know Him more and more.

4 So I'll wait a little longer, till His appointed time,
  And along the upward pathway my pilgrim feet shall climb;
  There, in my Father's dwelling, where many mansions be,
  I shall sweetly talk with Jesus, and He will talk with me.

No. 118. THE LORD'S PRAYER.

MARSHALL. By per.

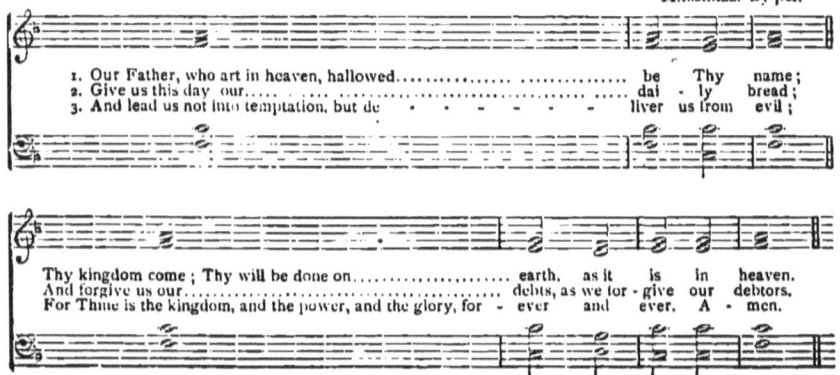

1. Our Father, who art in heaven, hallowed.................. be Thy name;
2. Give us this day our.................................... dai-ly bread;
3. And lead us not into temptation, but de — — — — — liver us from evil;

Thy kingdom come; Thy will be done on................ earth, as it is in heaven.
And forgive us our.................................... debts, as we for-give our debtors.
For Thine is the kingdom, and the power, and the glory, for - ever and ever. A-men.

108

No. 119. KEEP PRAYING AT THE DOOR.

"Seek, and ye shall find." — Philip Phillips.

1. Keep praying at the door, And knocking while you pray, Nor tremble, tho' the tempter's voice Would fright your soul away. Keep praying at the door, Still praying at the door; Tho' long the answer is delayed, Keep praying at the door.

2 The Lord will surely come,
His promise cannot fail;
O knock, and pray, and plead, and call,
Thy prayer will yet prevail.—*Ref.*

3 The door will open wide,
And thou shalt enter in,
And from the Holy One receive
A pardon for thy sin.—*Ref.*

No. 120. TEACH ME ALWAY.

Dr. L. W. Munhall. — *"Teach me Thy way, O Lord."* — D. B. Towner.

1. Ho-ly Spir-it, Teach-er Thou! In hu-mil-i-ty we bow; Come, perform Thine of-fice now, Teach me al-way.
2. Com-fort-er in deed Thou art, Speak to ev-'ry ach-ing heart; Let me nev-er from Thee part, Com-fort al-way.

2 Sent to be our Guide to-day,
Walking in the narrow way;
From it may we never stray,
Guide us alway.

4 Teacher, Comforter, and Guide,
Ever in our hearts abide;
And whatever may betide,
Help us alway.

No. 121. HOLY, HOLY! LORD GOD ALMIGHTY!

"They rest not day and night, saying, Holy, Holy, Lord God Almighty, which was, and is, and is to come."—REV. 4: 8.

REGINALD HEBER, D. D. REV. JOHN B. DYKES.

3 Holy, Holy, Holy! tho' the darkness hide thee,
Tho' the eye of sinful man Thy glory may not see,
Only Thou art Holy, there is none beside Thee
Perfect in power, in love, and purity.

4 Holy, Holy, Holy! Lord God Almighty!
All Thy works shall praise Thy name in earth, and sky, and sea;
Holy, Holy, Holy! Merciful and Mighty!
God in three Persons, blessed Trinity! Amen.

No. 122. CHILD OF SIN AND SORROW. 6s & 4s.

"Boast not of to-morrow."

THOMAS HASTINGS.

2 Child of sin and sorrow,
Why wilt thou die?
Come, while thou canst borrow
Help from on high:
Grieve not that love
Which from above,
Child of sin and sorrow,
Would bring thee nigh.

3 Child of sin and sorrow,
Thy moments glide,
Like the flitting arrow,
Or the rushing tide;
Ere time is o'er,
Heaven's grace implore;
Child of sin and sorrow
In Christ confide.

4 Child of sin and sorrow,
Where wilt thou be
Through that long to-morrow,
Eternity?
Exiled from home,
Darkly to roam,
Child of sin and sorrow,
Where wilt thou flee?

Thomas Hastings.

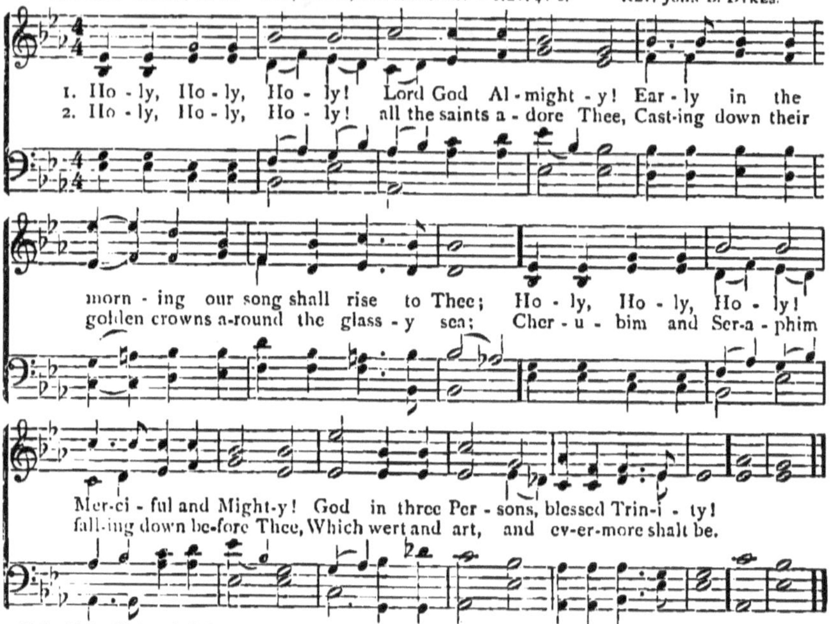

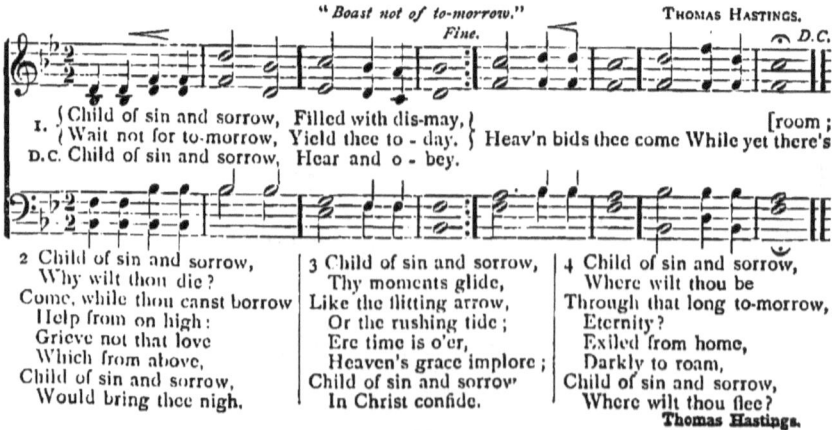

No. 123. HERALD ANGELS. 7s.

"*Glory to God in the highest.*"

Spirito. FELIX MENDELSSOHN.

1. Hark! the her-ald an-gels sing, "Glo-ry to the new born King! Peace on earth, and mer-cy mild; God and sin-ners rec-on-ciled." Joy-ful, all ye na-tions, rise; Join the triumph of the skies; With th'angel-ic hosts proclaim, "Christ is born in Beth-le-hem." Hark! the her-ald an-gels sing, "Glo-ry to the new-born King!"

2 Hail, the heaven-born Prince of Peace!
Hail, the Sun of Righteousness!
Light and life to all He brings,
Risen with healing in His wings.
Let us then with angels sing,
"Glory to the new-born King!
Peace on earth, and mercy mild
God and sinners reconciled!"
Hark! the herald angels, &c.

Charles Wesley.

No. 124. EVENING PRAYER. 8s & 7s.

D. BORTNIANSKY.

1. Sav - iour! breathe an eve - ning bless - ing, Ere re - pose our spir - its seal;
   Sin and want we come con - fess - ing, Thou canst save, and Thou canst heal.

Though the night be dark and drear - y, Dark - ness can - not hide from Thee;

Thou art He who, nev - er wea - ry, Watch-est where Thy peo - ple be.

2 Though destruction walk around us,
  Though the arrow past us fly,
  Angel guards from Thee surround us,
  We are safe if Thou art nigh.
  Should swift death this night o'ertake us,
  And our couch become our tomb,
  May the morn in heaven awake us,
  Clad in light and deathless bloom.
                                James Edmeston.

No. 125.

Sweet Hour of Prayer.
By permission.

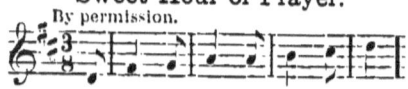

1 SWEET hour of prayer, sweet hour of prayer,
  That calls me from a world of care,
  And bids me, at my Father's throne,
  Make all my wants and wishes known!

In seasons of distress and grief,
My soul has often found relief,
And oft escaped the tempter's snare,
By thy return, sweet hour of prayer.

2 Sweet hour of prayer, sweet hour of prayer,
  Thy wings shall my petition bear
  To Him, whose truth and faithfulness
  Engage the waiting soul to bless:
  And since He bids me seek His face,
  Believe His word, and trust His grace,
  I'll cast on Him my every care,
  And wait for thee, sweet hour of prayer.

3 Sweet hour of prayer, sweet hour of prayer,
  May I thy consolation share,
  Till, from Mount Pisgah's lofty height,
  I view my home, and take my flight:
  This robe of flesh, I'll drop, and rise
  To seize the everlasting prize;
  And shout, while passing through the air,
  Farewell, farewell, sweet hour of prayer!

No. 126. TO JESUS I WILL GO.

"I will arise and go to my father."

F. J. Crosby. W. H. Doane. By per.

1. There's a gentle voice within calls a-way, 'Tis a warning I have heard o'er and o'er;
But my heart is melted now, I o-bey; From my Saviour I will wander no more.

CHORUS.
Yes, I will go; yes, I will go; To Jesus I will go and be saved;
Yes, I will go; yes, I will go; To Jesus I will go and be saved.

2 He has promised all my sins to forgive,
  If I ask in simple faith His love;
  In His holy word I learn how to live,
  And to labor for His kingdom above.—*Cho.*

3 I will try to bear the cross in my youth,
  And be faithful to its cause till I die;
  If with cheerful step I walk in the truth,
  I shall wear a starry crown by and by.—*Cho.*

4 Still the gentle voice within calls away,
  And its warning I have heard o'er and o'er;
  But my heart is melted now, I obey;
  From my Saviour I will wander no more.—*Cho.*

Copyright, 1869, in "Bright Jewels," by Biglow & Main Co.

No. 127.   BEHOLD THE BRIDEGROOM.

"*Behold, the bridegroom cometh; go ye out to meet Him.*"

R. E. Hudson.

1. Are you ready for the Bridegroom When He comes, when He comes? Are you
2. Have your lamps trimmed and burning, When He comes, when He comes; Have your

ready for the Bridegroom When He comes, when He comes? Be-hold! He com-eth! be-
lamps trimmed and burning When He comes, when He comes. He quick-ly com-eth! He

D. S. Be-hold! He cometh! be-

Fine. Chorus.

hold! He cometh! Be robed and ready, for the Bridegroom comes. Behold the Bridegroom,
quickly cometh, O soul, be ready when the Bridegroom comes.

hold! He cometh! Be robed and ready, for the Bridegroom comes.

D. S.

for He comes, for He comes! Behold the Bridegroom, for He comes, for He comes

3 ‖: We will all go out to meet Him
When He comes, when He comes ::‖
He surely cometh! He surely cometh!
We'll go to meet Him when the Bridegroom
comes.—*Cho.*

4 ‖: We will chant alleluias
When He comes, when He comes ::‖
Lo! now He cometh! lo! now He
cometh!
Sing alleluia, for the Bridegroom comes.—*Cho.*

No. 128. ONE SWEETLY SOLEMN THOUGHT.

"Now they desire a better country, that is, an heavenly." —Heb. 11: 16.

Miss Phoebe Carey. Philip Phillips.

1. One sweet - ly sol - emn thought Comes to me o'er and o'er; I'm near - er home to - day, to - day, Than I have been be - fore.

CHORUS.

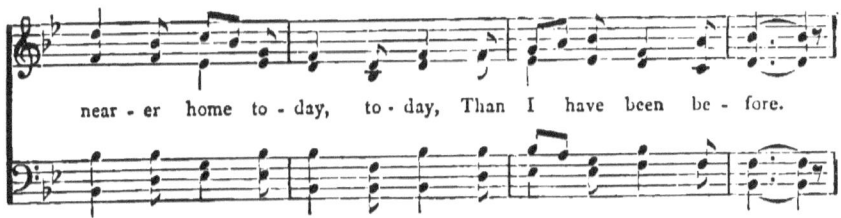

Nearer my home, Nearer my home, Nearer my home to-day, today, Than I have been before.

2 Nearer my Father's house,
  Where many mansions be;
  Nearer the great white throne to-day,
  Nearer the crystal sea.

3 Nearer the bound of life,
  Where burdens are laid down;
  Nearer to leave the cross to-day,
  And nearer to the crown.

4 Be near me when my feet
  Are slipping o'er the brink;
  For I am nearer home to-day,
  Perhaps, than now I think.

No. 129. STILL I AM SINGING.

"And he ministered with singing."

PHILIP PHILLIPS.

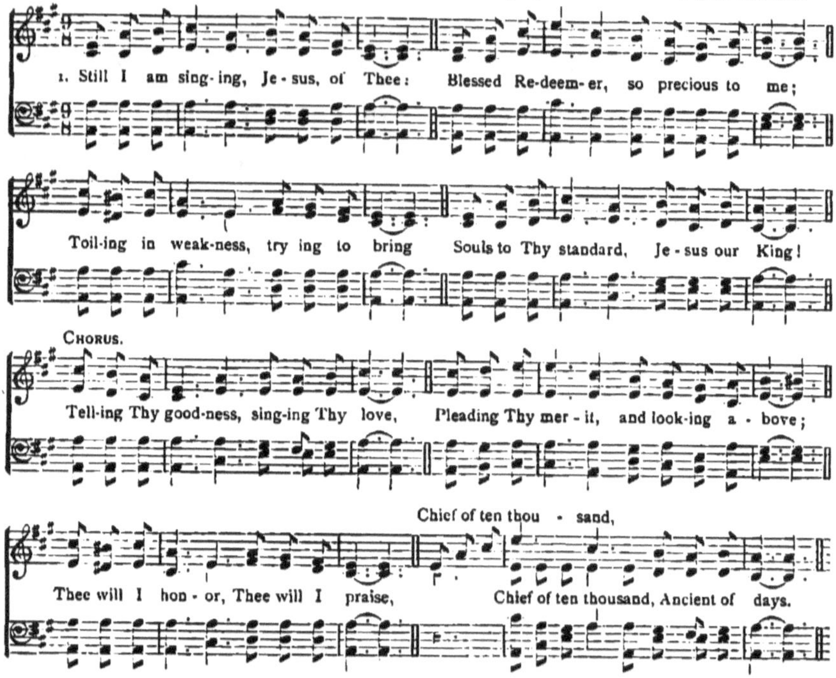
1. Still I am sing-ing, Je-sus, of Thee: Blessed Re-deem-er, so precious to me;
Toil-ing in weak-ness, try-ing to bring Souls to Thy standard, Je-sus our King!
CHORUS.
Tell-ing Thy good-ness, sing-ing Thy love, Pleading Thy mer-it, and look-ing a-bove;
Chief of ten thou-sand,
Thee will I hon-or, Thee will I praise, Chief of ten thousand, Ancient of days.

2 Still I am singing, Jesus, of Thee:
Simple the tones of the music may be;
Yet may the language comfort impart,
Lifting the spirit, cheering the heart.—*Cho.*

3 Still may our chorus joyfully be,
Blessed Redeemer, Hosanna to Thee:
Grant in Thy Kingdom all may unite,
Singing with rapture songs of delight.—*Cho.*

No. 130. TOSSING ON THE BILLOW.

"Both sure and steadfast."

S. J. VAIL.

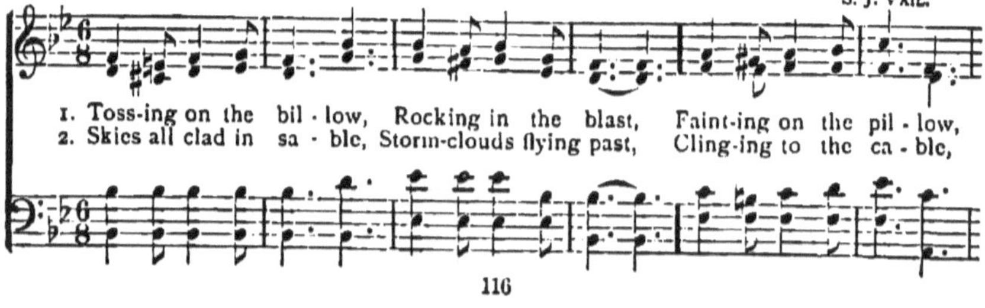
1. Toss-ing on the bil-low, Rocking in the blast, Faint-ing on the pil-low,
2. Skies all clad in sa-ble, Storm-clouds flying past, Cling-ing to the ca-ble,

TOSSING ON THE BILLOW. Concluded.

3 Gone each earthly treasure,
　Cut away each mast;
　Vanish earthly pleasure,
　Still I'm anchored fast. *Cho.*

4 Sorrows multiplying,
　Prospects overcast,
　Weeping, groaning, sighing,
　Still I'm anchored fast. *Cho.*

No. 131. FROM STORM ENTER INTO REST.

"*Enter in through the gates into the city.*" PHILIP PHILLIPS.

2 From hunger and from thirst,
　　Enter thy rest;
　From toil and weariness,
　　Enter thy rest.
　From shadows and from dreams,
　　Enter into rest;
　Enter into rest,
　　The rest of God.

3 From vanity and lies,
　　Enter thy rest;
　From mocking and from snares,
　　Enter thy rest.
　From disappointed hopes,
　　Enter into rest;
　Enter into rest,
　　The rest of God. Dr. H. Bonar.

No. 132.   HERE AND HEREAFTER.

"*For now we see through a glass darkly, but then face to face.*"

PHILIP PHILLIPS.

1. Life is but a fleet-ing dream, On-ly strangers here we roam;
Life is but a change-ful scene, Yon-der is the Christian's home.
Just be-yond the roll-ing tide An-gels watch us on the shore,
Where the pearl-y wa-ters glide, And the wear-y thirst no more.

2 Here we feel the tempter's power,
Here we sigh for living-bread,
Clouds of gloom and darkness lower,
While a rugged path we tread.
There no cruel thorns are found,
Doubt and fear and storms are o'er,
There the fruits of joy abound,
We shall hunger there no more.

3 Here we breathe the sultry air
Of a lonely desert plain,
Trials here the heart must bear
Worn by sickness, racked with pain.

There the waves of death are passed,
There, among the pure and blest,
Safely anchored home at last,
There our wandering feet shall rest.

4 Here our fondest hopes are brief,
Kindred ties are broken here;
Morning brings a night of grief,
Joy is mingled with a tear.
There shall faith be lost in sight,
There a long eternal day,
Christ the Lamb shall be the Light,
He will wipe our tears away.

No. 133. THE GOLDEN STORE.

"Behold, a sower went forth to sow."

P. Phillips.

2 Sun and shower aid thee now,
  Scatter seed!
Who can tell where grain may grow?
Winds are blowing to and fro,
Daily good thy simple creed.
Scatter, scatter goodly seed!—CHORUS.

3 Though thy work should seem to fail,
  Scatter seed!
Some may fall on stony ground:
Flower and blade are often found
In the clefts we little heed.
Scatter, scatter goodly seed!—CHORUS.

4 Springtime always dawns for thee!
  Scatter seed!
Open, then, thy golden store,
Stretch thy furrows more and more;
God will give thee all thy need.
Scatter, scatter goodly seed!—CHORUS.

No. 134. Blessed Bible, how I love it.

Tune "CLOSE TO THEE."

1 Blessed Bible, how I love it,
  How it doth my bosom cheer;
What on earth like this to covet,
  O what stores of wealth are here.

Cho. This my guide, this my guide,
  This my guide ever be:
All along my pilgrim journey,
  This my guide shall ever be!

2 Yes, sweet Bible! I will hide thee
  Deep, yes, deeper in this heart;
Thou through all my life wilt guide me,
  And in death we will not part.—*Cho.*

3 Part in death? no, never! never!
  Through death's vale I'll lean on thee;
Then in worlds above, for ever,
  Sweeter still thy truths shall be.—*Cho.*

Phebe Palmer.

No. 135.   THE CHRISTIAN WARFARE.

"*Fight the good fight of faith.*" Words and music by GEO. F. ROOT.

1. O, we are vol-un-teers in the ar-my of the Lord, Forming in-to line at our Cap-tain's word; We are un-der marching or-ders to take the bat-tle-field, And we'll ne'er give o'er the fight till the foe shall yield. Come, and join the ar-my, the ar-my of the Lord, Je-sus is our Cap-tain, we ral-ly at His word; Sharp will be the con-flict with the pow'rs of sin, But with such a Lead-er, we are sure to win.

2 The glory of our flag is the emblem of the dove,
 Gleaming are our swords from the forge of love ;
 We go forth, but not to battle for earthly honors vain,
 'Tis a bright immortal crown that we seek to gain.—*Cho.*

3 Our foes are in the field, pressing hard on ev'ry side,—
 Envy, anger, hatred, with self and pride ;
 They are cruel, fierce and strong, ever ready to attack ;
 We must watch, and fight, and pray, if we'd drive them back.—*Cho.*

4 O, glorious is the struggle in which we draw the sword,
 Glorious is the Kingdom of Christ, our Lord ;
 It shall spread from sea to sea, it shall reach from shore to shore,
 And His people shall be blessed for evermore.—*Cho.*

No. 136. WE SHALL SLEEP, BUT NOT FOR EVER.

Mrs. M. A. KIDDER. "*Sown in corruption...raised in incorruption.*" S. J. VAIL.

2 When we see a precious blossom
   That we tended with such care,
   Rudely taken from our bosom,
   How our aching hearts despair!
   Round its little grave we linger,
   Till the setting sun is low,
   Felling all our hopes have perished
   With the flower we cherished so.—*Cho.*

3 We shall sleep, but not for ever,
   In the lone and silent grave;
   Blessed be the Lord that taketh,
   Blessed be the Lord that gave.
   In the bright, eternal city
   Death can never, never come!
   In His own good time He'll call us
   From our rest to Home, sweet Home. *Cho.*

No. 137. WHAT SHALL IT PROFIT ME THEN?

"*What shall a man give in exchange for his soul?*"

FANNIE J. CROSBY.   S. J. VAIL.

2 What shall it profit me by-and-by—
O, what shall it profit me then?
Whether in weariness, toil and pain
I have been striving my home to gain—
Striving, not questioning how or why,
If I but rest with Him by-and-by?
Ref.—What shall it profit me then?
    What shall it profit me then?
    When I look back on it by-and-by,
    What shall it profit me then?

3 What shall it profit me by-and-by—
O, what shall it profit me then?
If I have answered the heavenly call,
Trusted in God as my all in all,

I shall be welcomed to dwell on high—
Dwell with the ransom'd ones by-and-by.
Ref.—‖: Thus shall it profit me then, :‖
    When I look back on it by-and-by,
    O, thus shall it profit me then.

4 What shall it profit me by-and-by—
O, what shall it profit me then?
Permit me this—That my gain and loss
Taught my weak spirit to bear the cross;
Bid me look upward to joys on high—
Heaven and happiness by-and-by.
Ref.—‖: Thus shall it profit me then, :‖
    When I look back on it by-and-by,
    O, thus shall it profit me then.

No. 138. WILL YOU GO WITH ME THERE.

"Sojourners and pilgrims."

S. J. Vail.

1. Why speeding so quick-ly, O Pil-grim? And where dost thou journey to - day?
Here rest thee a moment, and tell me, What need of such haste on the way?

Duet. I haste, for the moments are fly - ing, I go to a cit - y most fair,
My beau - ti - ful home o - ver Jor - dan; Then, say, will you go with me there?

Chorus. O haste to the cit - y most fair, 'Tis free from all sor - row and care;
Dear friends, in the vale o - ver Jor - dan, Are long - ing to wel-come us there.

2.
Solo. What! leave the gay pleasures around me,
The dance with its music and mirth,
The splendors of wealth that have bound me,
And wedded my spirit to earth?

Duet. Yes, leave them and cling to thy Saviour
Remember thy soul, and beware;
Thy soul, that by Him was created
A place in thy kingdom to share.—*Cho.*

3.
Solo. Will Jesus receive me, O pilgrim,
When long I have slighted His love,
Regarding the world as my treasure,
Forgetting the mansions above?

Duet. He waits even now to be gracious,
He waits in His mercy for thee ;
L ent from thy heart, and believe Him;
Then onward! rejoicing with me.—*Cho.*

No. 139. THE ROCK THAT IS HIGHER THAN I!

"*Lead me to the Rock that is higher than I.*"

E. Johnson.   W. G. Fischer.

2 O, sometimes how long seems the day,
And sometimes how heavy my feet!
But toiling in life's dusty way,
The Rock's blessed shadow, how sweet!

3 O, near to the Rock let me keep,
Though blessings or sorrows prevail;
When climbing the mountain-way steep,
Or walking the shadowy vale.

No. 141. ROCKED IN THE CRADLE OF THE DEEP.

"Then He arose, and rebuked the wind and the raging of the water." J. P. KNIGHT.

1. Rocked in.. the cradle of the deep,   I lay me down in peace to sleep;
2. And   such   the trust that still were mine, Tho' stormy winds swept o'er the brine;

Se-cure   I rest up-on the   wave, For Thou, O Lord,   hast power to save.
Or, tho' the tempest's fier-y   breath Rous'd me from sleep   to wreck and death,

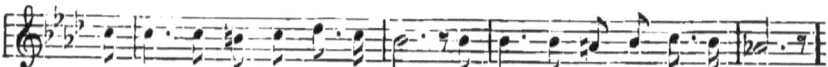

I know Thou wilt not slight my call, For Thou dost mark the sparrow's fall ;
In   o - cean's cave still safe with Thee, The germ of im - mor-tal - i - ty;

And calm and peaceful   is   my   sleep,   Rocked in   the cra-dle of the deep ;

And calm and peaceful   is   my   sleep,   Rocked in   the cra - dle   of   the deep.

No. 142. FOR THOSE AT SEA.

"And there was a calm."

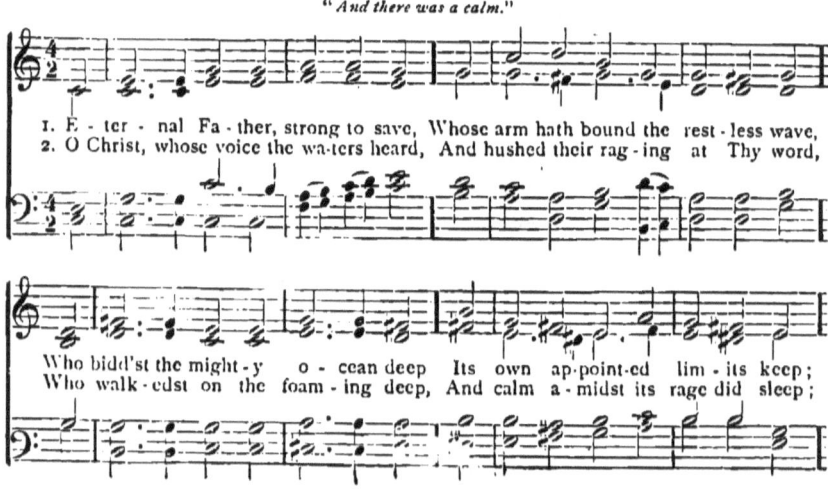

1. E - ter - nal Fa - ther, strong to save, Whose arm hath bound the rest - less wave,
2. O Christ, whose voice the wa-ters heard, And hushed their rag - ing   at Thy word,

Who bidd'st the might - y   o - cean deep Its   own ap-point-ed   lim - its keep;
Who walk - edst on the   foam - ing deep, And calm a - midst its rage did sleep;

No. 143. JESUS IS CALLING.

"To-day if ye will hear his voice." Geo. C. Stebbins.

1. Jesus is tenderly calling thee home—Calling to-day, calling to-day;
Why from the sunshine of love wilt thou roam, Farther and farther away?

REFRAIN.
Calling to-day, . . calling to-day. . .
Calling, calling to-day, to-day; Calling, calling to-day, to-day.
Jesus is calling, is tenderly calling to-day,
Jesus is tenderly calling to-day.

Copyright, 1883, by Geo. C. Stebbins.

2 Jesus is calling the weary to rest—
Calling to-day, calling to-day;
Bring him thy burden and thou shalt be blest;
He will not turn thee away.—REF.

3 Jesus is waiting, oh, come to him now—
Waiting to-day, waiting to-day;
Come with thy sins, at his feet lowly bow;
Come, and no longer delay.—REF.

4 Jesus is pleading, oh, list to his voice—
Hear him to-day, hear him to-day;
They who believe on his name shall rejoice;
Quickly arise and away.—REF.

FANNY J. CROSBY.

No. 144. LIKE THE FULLNESS OF THE SEA.

"*A broken and a contrite heart, O God, Thou wilt not despise.*"

S. J. VAIL.

1. There's a full-ness in God's mercy, Like the full-ness of the sea;
There's a kind-ness in His jus-tice Which is more than lib-er-ty.

REFRAIN.
He is call-ing, "Come to Me!" Lord, I'll glad-ly haste to Thee.

2 For the love of God is broader
  Than the measure of man's mind ;
  And the heart of the Eternal
  Is most wonderfully kind.—*Ref.*

3 Pining souls! come nearer Jesus ;
  Come, but come not doubting thus ;

Copyright, 1873, by Biglow & Main Co.

Come with faith that trusts more freely
His great tenderness for us.—*Ref.*

4 If our love were but more simple,
  We should take Him at His word ;
  And our lives would be all sunshine
  In the sweetness of our Lord.—*Ref.*

No. 145. I'M A PILGRIM.

Mrs. S. B. DANA. "*Here we have no continuing city.*" I. B. WOODBURY.

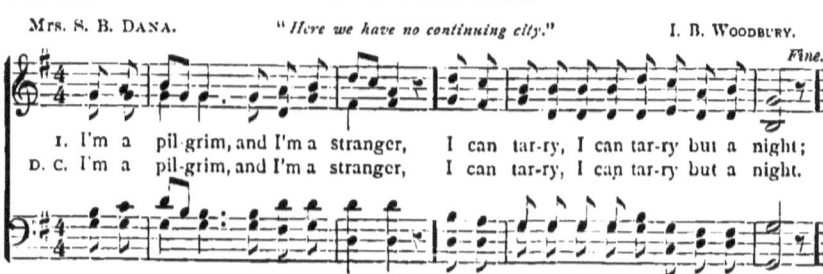

1. I'm a pil-grim, and I'm a stranger, I can tar-ry, I can tar-ry but a night;
D.C. I'm a pil-grim, and I'm a stranger, I can tar-ry, I can tar-ry but a night.

I'M A PILGRIM. Concluded.

Do not de-tain me, for I am go-ing To where the fountains are ev-er flow-ing.

2 There the glory is ever shining;
I am longing, I am longing for the sight;
Here in this country, so dark and dreary,
I have been wand'ring forlorn and weary.
I'm a pilgrim and I'm a stranger;
I can tarry, I can tarry but a night.

3 There's the city to which I journey;
My Redeemer, my Redeemer is its light;
There is no sorrow, nor any sighing,
There is no sin there, nor any dying.
I'm a pilgrim, and I'm a stranger;
I can tarry, I can tarry but a night.

No. 146. GOD SPEED THE RIGHT.

"*And every man that striveth for the mastery is temperate in all things.*"

With Spirit. W. E. HICKSON. From the German.

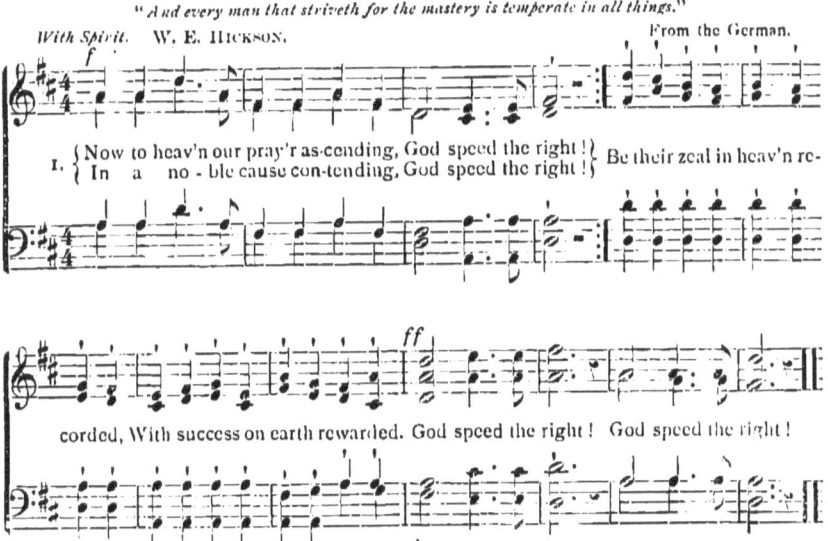

1. { Now to heav'n our pray'r as-cending, God speed the right!
   { In a no-ble cause con-tending, God speed the right! } Be their zeal in heav'n re-

corded, With success on earth rewarded. God speed the right! God speed the right!

2 Be that prayer again repeated,
  God speed the right!
Ne'er despairing, though defeated,
  God speed the right!
Like the good and great in story,
If they fall, they fall with glory.
  God speed the right!

3 Patient, firm, and persevering,
  God speed the right!
Ne'er the event our danger fearing,
  God speed the right!
Pains, nor toils, nor trials heeding,
And in heaven's own time succeeding.
  God speed the right!

No. 147. A LAND WITHOUT A STORM.

"A better country."   Arr. by WM. B. BRADBURY.

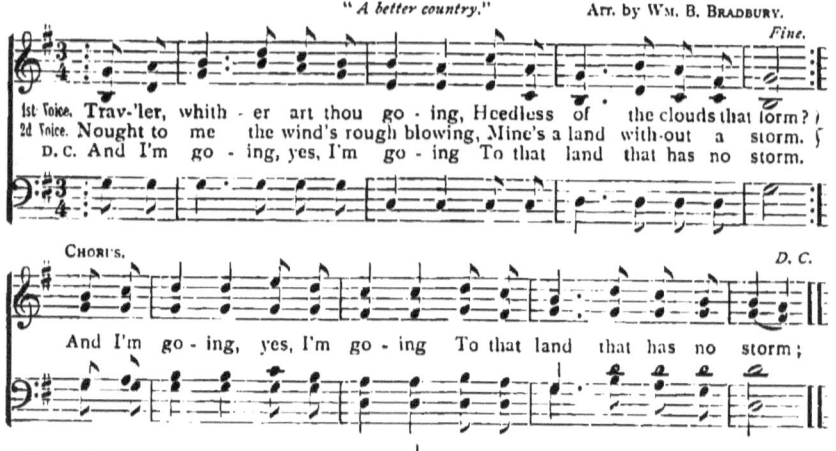

1st Voice. Trav-'ler, whith-er art thou go-ing, Heedless of the clouds that form?
2d Voice. Nought to me the wind's rough blowing, Mine's a land with-out a storm.
D. C. And I'm go-ing, yes, I'm go-ing To that land that has no storm.

CHORUS.

And I'm go-ing, yes, I'm go-ing To that land that has no storm;

1st Voice. 2 Trav'ler, art thou here a stranger,
    Not to fear the tempest's power?
2d Voice.   I have not a thought of danger,
    Tho' the sky may darkly lower.

1st Voice. 3 Trav'ler, now a moment linger,
    Soon the darkness will be o'er.

2d Voice. No! I see a beckoning finger,
    Guiding to a far-off shore.
1st Voice. 4 Trav'ler, yonder narrow portal
    Opens to receive thy form.
2d Voice. Yes, but I shall be immortal
    In that land without a storm.

Copyright, 1861, by W. B. Bradbury.

No. 148. GOD IS OUR REFUGE.

"A very present help in trouble."   Dr. L. MASON.

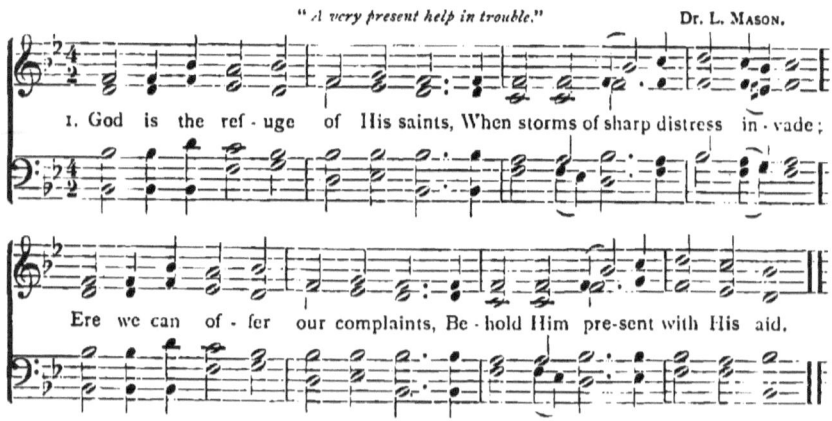

1. God is the ref-uge of His saints, When storms of sharp distress in-vade;
Ere we can of-fer our complaints, Be-hold Him pre-sent with His aid.

2 Loud may the troubled ocean roar,
    In sacred peace our souls abide;
While every nation, every shore,
    Trembles and dreads the swelling tide.

3 There is a stream whose gentle flow
    Supplies the city of our God;

Life, love, and joy still gliding through,
    And watering our divine abode.

4 That sacred stream, Thy holy Word,
    Supports our faith, our fear controls;
Sweet peace Thy promises afford,
    And give new strength to fainting souls.

No. 149. YOUR MISSION.

"*Whatsoever thy hand findeth to do, do it with thy might.*"

Mrs. Ellen H. Gates. Vail and Phillips.

3 If you have not gold and silver
   Ever ready to command ;
   If you cannot tow'rds the needy
   Reach an ever-open hand ;
   You can visit the afflicted,
   O'er the erring you can weep,
   You can be a true disciple,
   Sitting at the Saviour's feet.
   Ref.—Sitting at the Saviour's, etc.

4 If you cannot in the conflict
   Prove yourself a soldier true ;
   If, where fire and smoke are thickest,
   There's no work for you to do ;
   When the battle-field is silent,
   You can go with careful tread,
   You can bear away the wounded,
   You can cover up the dead.
   Ref.—You can cover, etc.

5 If you cannot in the harvest
   Garner up the richest sheaves,
   Many a grain both ripe and golden
   Will the careless reapers leave ;
   Go and glean among the briars,
   Growing rank against the wall,
   For it may be that their shadow
   Hides the heaviest wheat of all.
   Ref.—Hides the heaviest, etc.

6 Do not, then, stand idly waiting
   For some greater work to do ;
   Fortune is a lazy goddess,
   She will never come to you.
   Go, and toil in any vineyard,
   Do not fear to do or dare ;
   If you want a field of labor,
   You can find it anywhere.
   Ref.—You can find, etc.

No. 150. BRIGHT HOME.

"In my Father's house are many mansions." H. R. BISHOP, 1816

1. Bright home of our Saviour, what glo-ries a-wait
   The spir-its that pass thro' thy bright pearl-y [OMIT] gate;
   What an-thems of rap-ture, un-
   Com-pose the loud cho-rus that ceasing and high,
   gladdens the [OMIT] sky! Home, home! sweet, sweet home! Prepare me, dear Saviour, for yonder blest home.

2 The home that our Saviour has gone to prepare—
  No heart can conceive of the blessedness there,
  Of raptures unending awaiting the just,
  When, pure in His likeness, they rise from the dust.   Home, etc.

3 We bless Thee, dear Saviour, who call'st us to share
  The beautiful home Thou hast gone to prepare;
  We trust in Thy mercy, that, washed from our sin,
  Through yonder bright gates we may all enter in.   Home, etc.

No. 151. HOLY SPIRIT, FAITHFUL GUIDE.

M. M. WELLS.

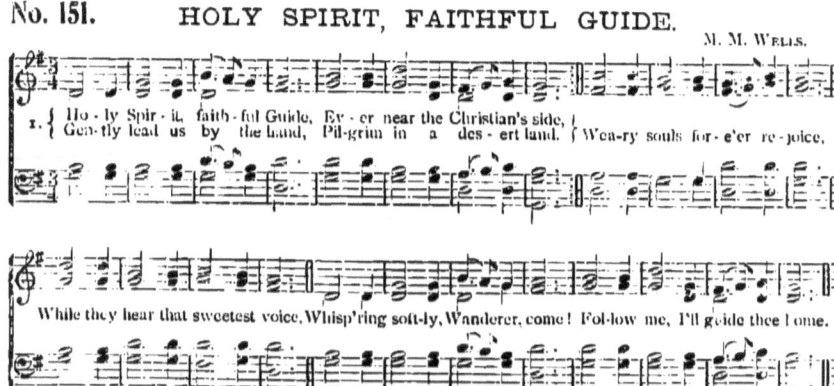

1. Ho-ly Spir-it, faith-ful Guide, Ev-er near the Christian's side,
   Gen-tly lead us by the hand, Pil-grim in a des-ert land.
   Wea-ry souls for-e'er re-joice,
   While they hear that sweetest voice, Whisp'ring soft-ly, Wanderer, come! Fol-low me, I'll guide thee home.

2 Ever-present, truest Friend,
  Ever near, Thine aid to lend,
  Leave us not to doubt and fear,
  Groping on in darkness drear.
  When the storms are raging sore,
  Hearts grow faint, and hopes give o'er,
  Whisper softly, Wanderer, come!
  Follow me, I'll guide thee home.

3 When our days of toil shall cease,
  Waiting still for sweet release,
  Nothing left but heaven and prayer,
  Wond'ring if our names are there;
  Wading deep the dismal flood,
  Pleading naught but Jesus' blood;
  Whisper softly, Wanderer, come!
  Follow me, I'll guide thee home.

No. 152.   O, BE SAVED!

F. J. Crosby "The Lord ready to save."   S. J. Vail, by per.

3 Jesus now is bending o'er thee,
     Jesus lowly, meek, and mild ;
   To the Friend who died to save thee,
     Wilt thou not be reconciled ?—Cho.
3 Art thou waiting till the morrow?
     Thou may'st never see its light ;
   Come at once ! accept His mercy ;
     He is waiting—come to night !—Cho.

Copyright, 1874, in "Songs of Grace and Glory."

4 With a lowly, contrite spirit,
     Kneeling at the Saviour's feet,
   Thou canst feel, this very moment,
     Pardon, precious, pure, and sweet !—Cho
5 Let the angels bear the tidings
     Upward to the courts of heaven !
   Let them sing, with holy rapture,
     O'er another soul forgiven !—Cho.

No. 153.   COME, COME TO JESUS!

Hubert P. Main.

1 Come, come to Jesus !
   He waits to welcome thee,
   O wand'rer, eagerly
   Come, come to Jesus !
2 Come, come to Jesus !
   He waits to ransom thee,
   O slave ! so willingly ;
   Come, come to Jesus !

3 Come, come to Jesus !
   He waits to lighten thee.
   O burdened ! trustingly
   Come, come to Jesus !
· Come, come to Jesus !
   He waits to give to thee,
   O blind ! a vision free ;
   Come, come to Jesus !

5 Come, come to Jesus !
   He waits to shelter thee ;
   O weary, blessedly
   Come, come to Jesus !
6 Come, come to Jesus !
   He waits to carry thee ;
   O lamb ! so lovingly,
   Come, come to Jesus !

No. 154. COME, THOU FOUNT OF EVERY BLESSING.

DR. NETTLETON.

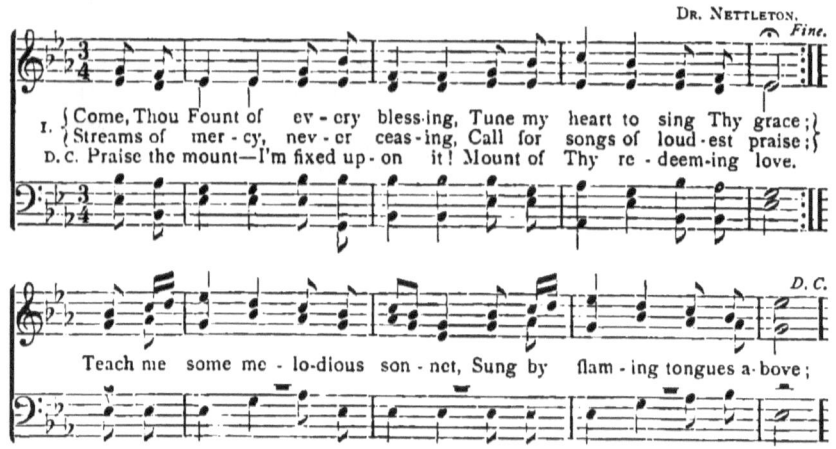

1. { Come, Thou Fount of ev-ery bless-ing, Tune my heart to sing Thy grace; }
   { Streams of mer-cy, nev-er ceas-ing, Call for songs of loud-est praise; }
D.C. Praise the mount—I'm fixed up-on it! Mount of Thy re-deem-ing love.

Teach me some me-lo-dious son-net, Sung by flam-ing tongues a-bove;

2 Here I raise my Ebenezer,
Hither by Thy help I'm come;
And I hope, by Thy good pleasure,
Safely to arrive at home.
Jesus sought me when a stranger,
Wandering from the fold of God,
He to rescue me from danger,
Interposed His precious blood.

3 Oh, to grace how great a debtor,
Daily I'm constrained to be!
Let Thy goodness, as a fetter,
Bind my wandering heart to Thee.
Prone to wander, Lord, I feel it—
Prone to leave the God I love—
Here's my heart, oh, take and seal it.
Seal it for Thy courts above.
Robinson.

No. 155. HEBRON.

"*Praise ye the Lord, for it is good to sing praises unto our God.*" L. MASON.

1. New every morning is Thy love, Thro' sleep and darkness safely brought,
Our waking and our rising prove; Returned to life, and power, and thought.

2 New mercies, each returning day,
Hover around us while we pray,
New perils past, new sins forgiven,
New thoughts of God, new hopes of heaven.

3 The trivial round, the common task,
Will furnish all we ought to ask,
Room to deny ourselves; a road
To bring us daily nearer God.

4 Only, O Lord, in Thy dear love,
Fit us for perfect rest above,
And help us this and every day,
To live more nearly as we pray.
Keble.

No. 156. The Lord Has Led Me.

1 Thus far the Lord has led me on,
Thus far His power prolongs my days,
And every evening shall make known
Some fresh memorial of His grace.

2 Much of my time has run to waste,
And I, perhaps, am near my home;
But He forgives my follies past,
And gives me strength for days to come.

3 I lay my body down to sleep;
Peace is the pillow for my head;
While well-appointed angels keep
Their watchful stations round my bed.
Watts.

No. 159.   CHRISTMAS.

No. 160.   JESUS, MY JOY.

Words by Mrs. J. F. CREWDSON.   Music by W. J. KIRKPATRICK, by per.

1. I've found a joy in sor-row, A se-cret balm for pain,
2. I've found a branch for heal-ing Near ev-'ry bit-ter spring,
3. I've found a glad ho-san-na For ev-'ry woe and wail,
4. I've found the Rock of A-ges When des-ert wells are dry;

A beau-ti-ful to-mor-row Of sun-shine af-ter rain.
A whis-pered prom-ise steal-ing O'er ev-'ry bro-ken string.
A hand-ful of sweet man-na When grapes of Es-chol fail.
And af-ter wea-ry sta-ges I've found an E-lim nigh.

CHORUS.
'Tis Je-sus, my por-tion for-ev-er, 'Tis Je-sus, the First and the Last;
A help ver-y pres-ent in trou-ble, A shel-ter from ev-'ry blast.

5 An Elim with its coolness,
    Its fountains, and its shade;
    A blessing in its fulness
    When buds of promise fade.

6 O'er tears of soft contrition
    I've seen a rainbow light:
    A glory and fruition,
    So near yet out of sight.

Copyright, 1873, by Wm. J. Kirkpatrick.

No. 161. PRECIOUS BLOOD OF CALVARY.

E. E. Hewitt.   Wm. J. Kirkpatrick, by per.

1. Bless - ed stream from Cal-v'ry's hill, Flow - ing free - ly, flow - ing still,
2. Shed, to take my sin a - way, Shed, to cleanse me day by day;
3. Though the whole wide world should come, At this foun - tain there is room;
4. When with all the saints a - bove, Saved, I sing re - deem-ing love,

Plunge me, Lord, be - neath the tide, Flowing from Thy riv - en side.
Sprink-ling now the mer - cy - seat, There I find com-mun - ion sweet.
Mil - lions at the cross I see, Yet He makes a place for me.
Still the blood my theme shall be, Shed for ma - ny, shed for me.

CHORUS.

Pre - cious blood of Cal - va - ry, Shed for ma - ny, shed for me.
This my all a - vail - ing plea, Je - sus shed His blood for me.

Copyright, 1894, W. J. Kirkpatrick.

No. 162. THE CHRISTMAS ARMY.

W. L. M. W. L. MASON.

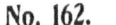

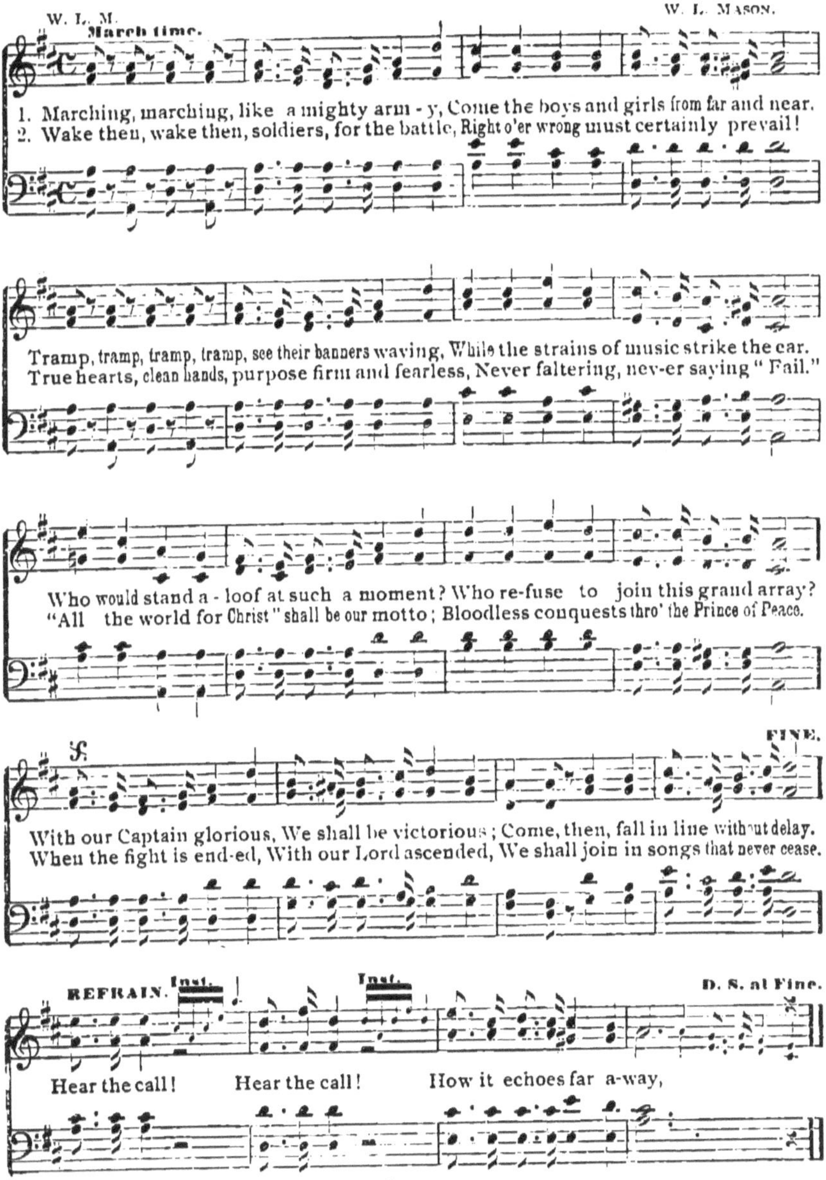

No. 165. DELIVERANCE WILL COME.

J. B. M.
REV. JNO. B. MATTHIAS, 1836.

1. I saw a way-worn trav-'ler In tat-ter'd gar-ments clad, His back was la-den heav-y, His strength was al-most gone,
2. The sum-mer sun was shin-ing, The sweat was on his brow, But he kept press-ing on-ward, For he was wend-ing home;
3. The song-sters in the ar-bor, That stood be-side the way, His watchword be-ing "On-ward!" He stopped his ears and ran,

And strug-gling up the moun-tain It seem'd that he was sad;
Yet he shout-ed as he journeyed, De-liv-er-ance will come.
His gar-ments worn and dust-y, His step seem'd ver-y slow:
Still shout-ing as he journeyed, De-liv-er-ance will come.
At-tract-ed his at-ten-tion, In-vit-ing his de-lay:
Still shout-ing as he journeyed, De-liv-er-ance will come.

CHORUS.

Then palms of vic-to-ry, crowns of glory, Palms of vic-to-ry I shall bear.

4 I saw him in the evening,
The sun was bending low,
He'd overtopped the mountain,
And reached the vale below:
He saw the golden city,—
His everlasting home,—
And shouted loud, Hosanna,
Deliverance will come!

5 While gazing on that city,
Just o'er the narrow flood,
A band of holy angels
Came from the throne of God:

They bore him on their pinions
Safe o'er the dashing foam;
And joined him in his triumph,—
Deliverance had come!

6 I heard the song of triumph
They sang upon that shore,
Saying, Jesus has redeemed us
To suffer nevermore;
Then, casting his eyes backward
On the race which he had run,
He shouted loud, Hosanna,
Deliverance has come!

No. 166. NOT HALF HAS EVER BEEN TOLD.

"And the building of the wall of it was of jasper; and the city was pure gold, like unto clear glass."—Rev. 21: 18.

REV. J. B. ATCHINSON.   O. F. PRESBREY. By per.

NOT HALF HAS EVER BEEN TOLD. Concluded.

145

No. 167. HIM THAT COMETH UNTO ME.

E. E. HEWITT.   John vi. 37.   WM. J. KIRKPATRICK, by per.

1. Lis-ten to the blessed in-vi-ta-tion, Sweeter than the notes of an-gel-song,
2. Wea-ry toil-er, sad and heav-y-la-den, Joy-ful-ly the great sal-va-tion see,
3. Come, ye thirst-y, to the liv-ing wa-ters, Hungry, come and on His bounty feed,

Chim-ing soft-ly with a heav'nly ca-dence, Call-ing to the pass-ing throng.
Close beside thee stands the Burden Bear-er, Strong to bear thy load and thee.
Not thy fit-ness is the plea to bring Him, But thy pressing ut-most need.

CHORUS.

Him that com-eth un-to me, un-to me, Him that com-eth un-to me, un-to me,
Him that com-eth un-to me, un-to me, I will in no wise cast out.

4 "Him that cometh," blind or maimed or sinful,
Cometh for His healing touch divine.
For the cleansing of the blood so precious,
Prove anew this gracious line.

5 Coming humbly, daily to this Saviour,
Breathing all the heart to Him in prayer;
Coming some day to the heavenly mansions,
He will give thee welcome there.

Copyright, 1888, by W. J. Kirkpatrick.

HAPPY IN THEE. Concluded.

spir - it is free, And oh, I am hap - py, dear Sav-iour, in Thee.

No. 170.　　　　　HALLELUJAH.
WM. G. COLLINS.　　　　　　　　　　　WM. J. KIRKPATRICK, by per.

1. I am glad; O so glad That to Je - sus I came. He has pardoned my
2. Oh, the ful - ness of joy My Re-deem - er to know, And to feel that His
3. Per - fect peace in my heart Je - sus now gives to me, From all fear - ing and
4. Sav-iour, keep me I pray, Ev - er keep me Thine own, Till I join the glad

CHORUS.

sins, I can now praise His Name. Hal - le - lu - jah, Je - sus saves me, With a
blood Makes me whit - er than snow.
doubt - ing, My spir - it is free.
song, Of the blest 'round Thy throne.

per - fect sal - va - tion, Hal - le - lu - jah, hal - le - lu - jah, Je-sus saves me just now.

Copyright, 1885, by Wm. J. Kirkpatrick.

AN OPEN BIBLE. Concluded.

No. 172.   FOLLOW ALL THE WAY.

GEO. W. COLLINS.   Arr. by WM. J. KIRKPATRICK, by per.

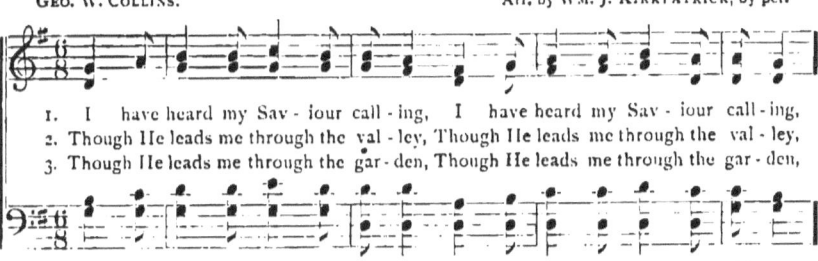

1. I have heard my Sav-iour call-ing, I have heard my Sav-iour call-ing,
2. Though He leads me through the val-ley, Though He leads me through the val-ley,
3. Though He leads me through the gar-den, Though He leads me through the gar-den,

CHO.—*Where He leads me I will fol-low, Where He leads me I will fol-low,*

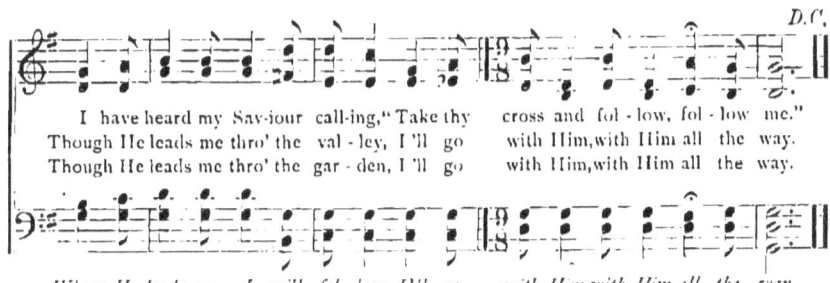

I have heard my Sav-iour call-ing," Take thy cross and fol-low, fol-low me."
Though He leads me thro' the val-ley, I'll go with Him, with Him all the way.
Though He leads me thro' the gar-den, I'll go with Him, with Him all the way.

Where He leads me I will fol-low, I'll go   with Him, with Him all the way.

4 |: Though the path be dark and dreary,:|
   I'll go with Him, with Him all the way.

5 |: Though He leads me in the conflict,:|
   I'll go with Him, with Him all the way.

6 |: Though He leads through fiery trial,:|
   I'll go with Him, with Him all the way.

7 |: I will follow on to know Him,:|
   He's my Saviour, Saviour, Brother, Friend.

8 |: He will give me grace and glory,:|
   He will keep me, keep me all the way.

9 |: O 't is sweet to follow Jesus,:|
   And be with Him, with Him all the way.

Copyright, 1891, by Wm. J. Kirkpatrick.

No. 174. PLEADING WITH THEE.

J. JACKSON. WM. J. KIRKPATRICK, by per.

1. Wea-ry, oh, yes, thou art wea-ry, Bear-ing thy bur-den of sin;
2. Lone-ly, oh, yes, thou art lone-ly, Plod-ding thy des-o-late way,
3. Trou-bled, oh, yes, thou art trou-bled, Com-fort has flown from thy breast;
4. Wea-ry and lone-ly and trou-bled, Bro-ken in spir-it and heart,

Clouds of the night are a-bove thee, Fear and temp-ta-tion with-in.
Far from the arms that would shield thee, Far from the light and the day.
On-ly in Je-sus thy ref-uge, On-ly in Him is thy rest.
Come to the gra-cious Re-deem-er: Child of His mer-cy thou art.

CHORUS.

Hear the sweet voice that is plead-ing with thee, Pleading with thee, pleading with thee,

Hear the sweet voice that is plead-ing with thee, Ten-der-ly plead-ing with thee.
Plead - - - ing with thee.

No. 175. I'VE FOUND THE PEARL.

Lowell Mason. (1792—1872.) 1830.

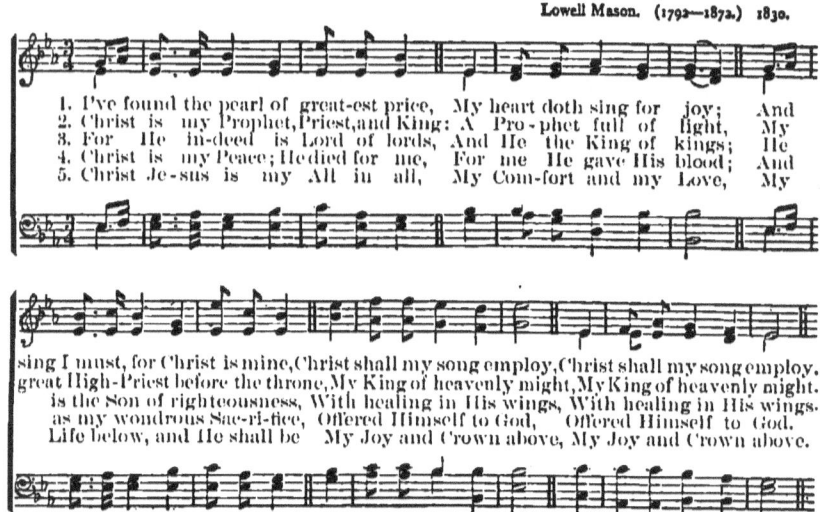

1. I've found the pearl of great-est price, My heart doth sing for joy; And sing I must, for Christ is mine, Christ shall my song employ, Christ shall my song employ.
2. Christ is my Prophet, Priest, and King: A Pro-phet full of light, My great High-Priest before the throne, My King of heavenly might, My King of heavenly might.
3. For He in-deed is Lord of lords, And He the King of kings; He is the Son of righteousness, With healing in His wings, With healing in His wings.
4. Christ is my Peace; He died for me, For me He gave His blood; And as my wondrous Sac-ri-fice, Offered Himself to God, Offered Himself to God.
5. Christ Je-sus is my All in all, My Com-fort and my Love, My Life below, and He shall be My Joy and Crown above, My Joy and Crown above.

No. 176. ROCKINGHAM. L. M.

Dr. L. Mason.

"*And rested the Sabbath-day.*"

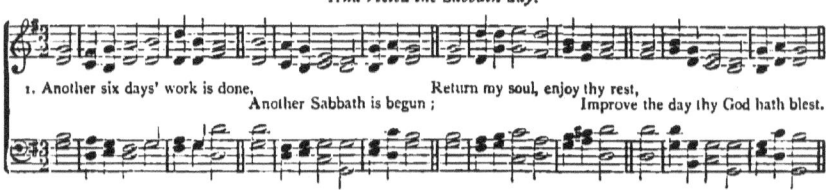

1. Another six days' work is done, Another Sabbath is begun; Return my soul, enjoy thy rest, Improve the day thy God hath blest.

2 Come, bless the Lord, whose love assigns
So sweet a rest to wearied minds;
Provides an antepast of heaven,
And gives this day the food of seven.

3 This heavenly calm within the breast,
Is the dear pledge of glorious rest,
Which for the church of God remains,
The end of cares, the end of pains.

4 O that our thoughts and thanks may rise,
As grateful incense to the skies;
And draw from heaven that sweet repose,
Which none but he that feels it knows.

5 In holy duties let the day
In holy pleasures pass away.
How blest a Sabbath thus to spend,
In hope of one that ne'er shall end.

Stennett.

No. 177. Sweet is the Light.

1 Sweet is the light of Sabbath eve,
And soft the sunbeams lingering there:
For these blest hours the world I leave,
Wafted on wings of faith and prayer.

2 The time—how lovely and how still;
Peace shines and smiles on all below;
The plain, the stream, the wood, the hill,
All fair with evening's setting glow.

3 Nor will our days of toil be long,
Our pilgrimage will soon be trod;
And we shall join the ceaseless song—
The endless Sabbath of our God.

James Edmeston.

No. 178.   COME, HOLY SPIRIT.

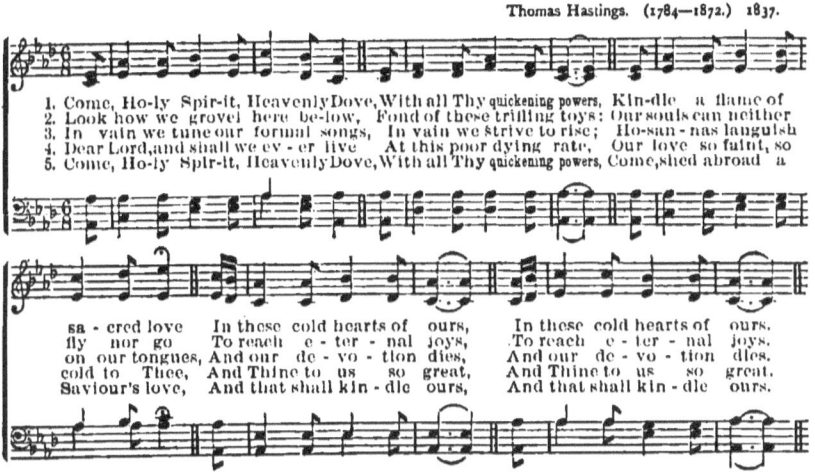

No. 179.   EASTER DAY. L. M.

"*I know that my Redeemer liveth.*"   PHILIP PHILLIPS.

2 He lives, to bless me with His love;
He lives, to plead for me above;
He lives, my hungry soul to feed;
He lives, to help in time of need.

3 He lives! all glory to His Name;
He lives! my Saviour, still the same;
What joy the blest assurance gives,—
I know that my Redeemer lives.

4 He lives! my wise and mighty friend;
He lives and loves me to the end;
He lives, my mansion to prepare;
He lives, to guide me safely there.
                      Wesley.

No. 180.   Easter Evening.

1 He dies! the friend of sinners dies;
Lo! Salem's daughters weep around;
A solemn darkness veils the skies,
A sudden trembling shakes the ground.

2 The rising God forsakes the tomb;
In vain the tomb forbids him rise!
Cherubic legions guard Him home,
And shout him welcome to the skies.

3 Say, "Live for ever, wondrous King,
Born to redeem, and strong to save;"
Then ask the monster,"Where's thy sting?
And where's thy vict'ry, boasting grave?"   Watts.

No. 184. THE SPIRIT, IN OUR HEARTS.

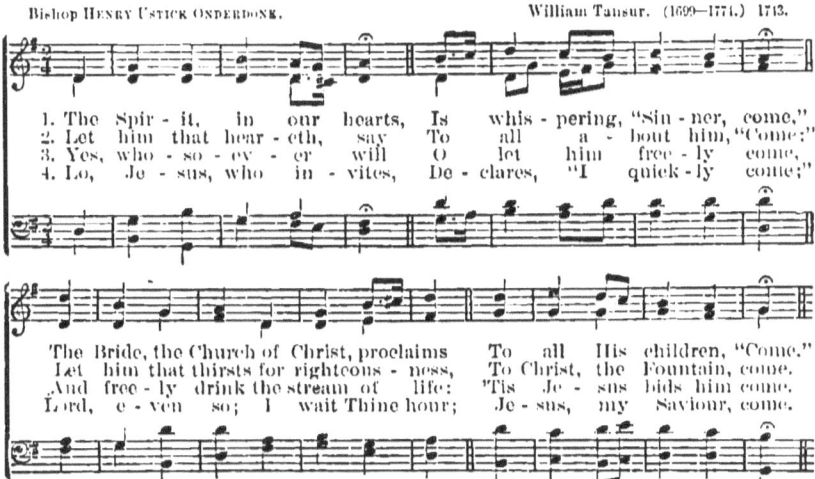

No. 185. COME, THOU ALMIGHTY KING.

Felice Giardini. (1716—1796.) 1760.

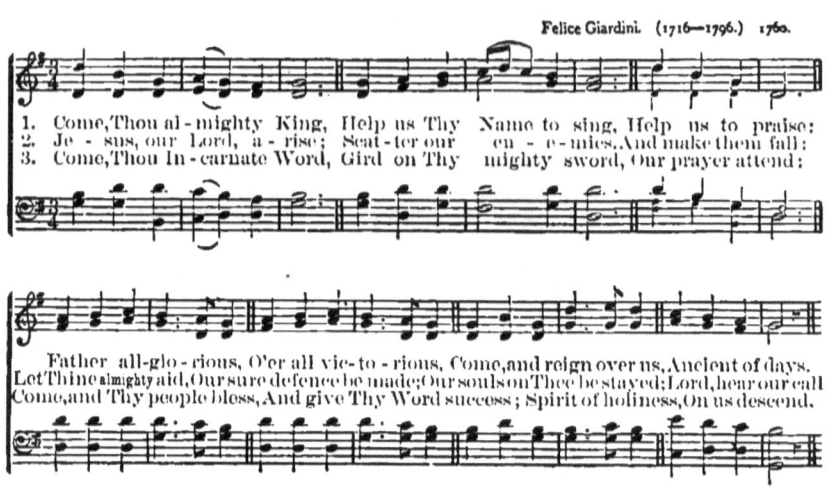

1. Come, Thou al-mighty King, Help us Thy Name to sing, Help us to praise:
2. Je-sus, our Lord, a-rise; Scat-ter our en-e-mies, And make them fall:
3. Come, Thou In-carnate Word, Gird on Thy mighty sword, Our prayer attend:

Father all-glo-rious, O'er all vic-to-rious, Come, and reign over us, Ancient of days.
Let Thine almighty aid, Our sure defence be made; Our souls on Thee be stayed; Lord, hear our call
Come, and Thy people bless, And give Thy Word success; Spirit of holiness, On us descend.

No. 186. MEAN MAY SEEM THIS HOUSE OF CLAY.

Isaac Beverly Woodbury. (1819—1858.) 1842.

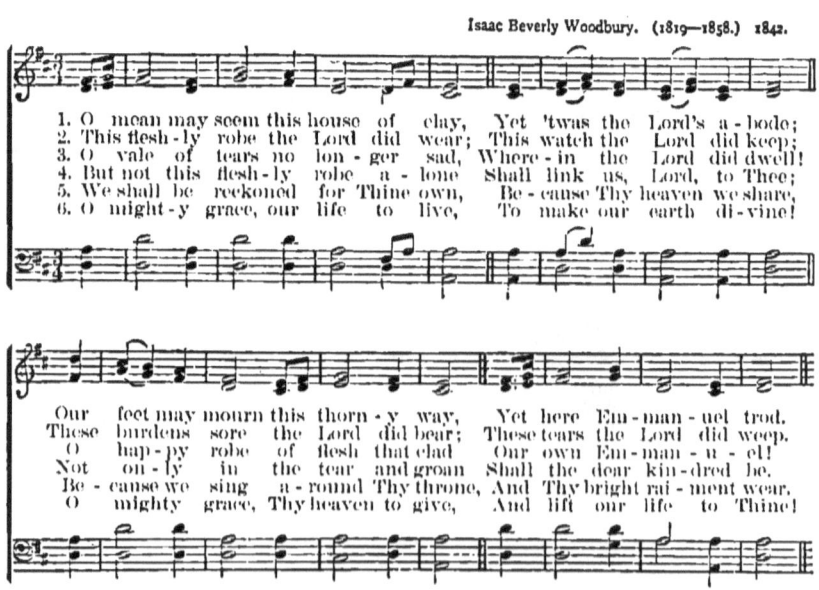

1. O mean may seem this house of clay, Yet 'twas the Lord's a-bode;
2. This flesh-ly robe the Lord did wear; This watch the Lord did keep;
3. O vale of tears no lon-ger sad, Where-in the Lord did dwell!
4. But not this flesh-ly robe a-lone Shall link us, Lord, to Thee!
5. We shall be reckoned for Thine own, Be-cause Thy heaven we share,
6. O might-y grace, our life to live, To make our earth di-vine!

Our feet may mourn this thorn-y way, Yet here Em-man-uel trod.
These burdens sore the Lord did bear; These tears the Lord did weep.
O hap-py robe of flesh that clad Our own Em-man-u-el!
Not on-ly in the tear and groan Shall the dear kin-dred be.
Be-cause we sing a-round Thy throne, And Thy bright rai-ment wear,
O mighty grace, Thy heaven to give, And lift our life to Thine!

No. 187. O DAY OF REST AND GLADNESS.

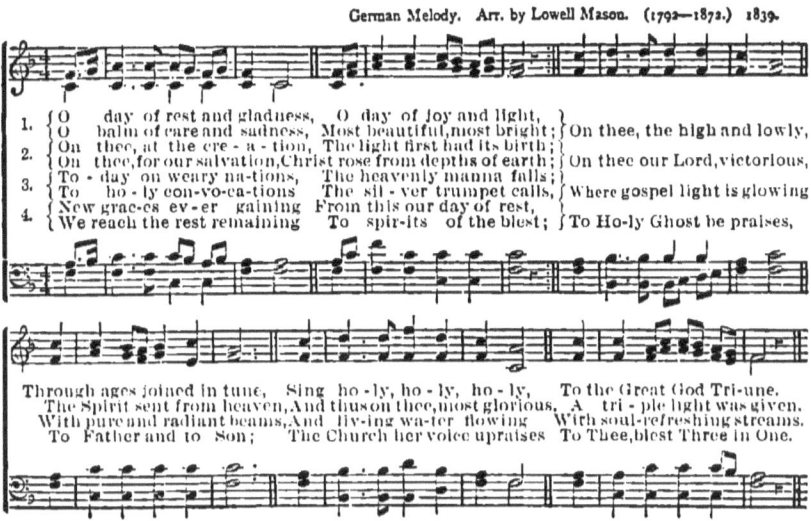

No. 188. SUN OF MY SOUL.

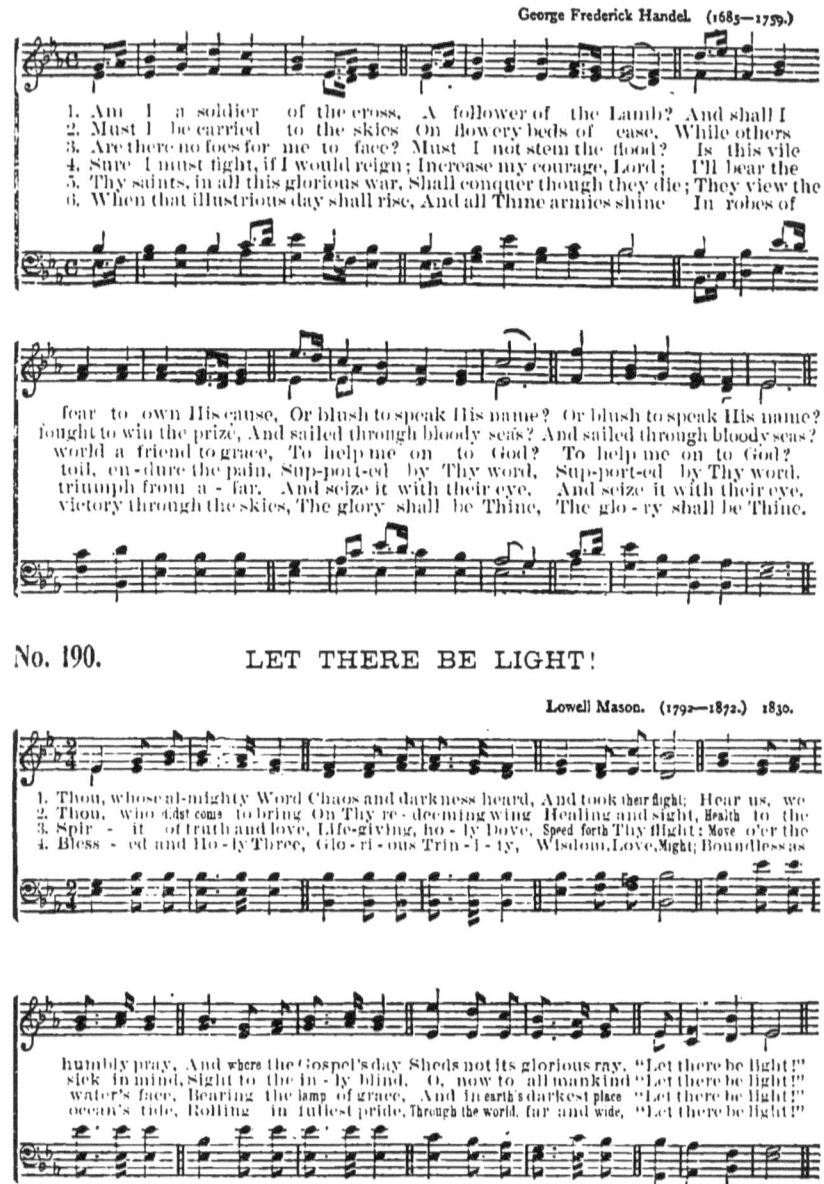

No. 191. JESUS, WHERE'ER THY PEOPLE MEET. L. M.

Lowell Mason. 1832.

1. Je-sus, where'er Thy peo-ple meet, There they be-hold Thy mer-cy-seat;
2. For Thou, within no walls confined, In-hab-it-est the humble mind;
3. Dear Shepherd of Thy cho-sen few, Thy for-mer mer-cies here re-new;
4. Here may we prove the power of prayer To strengthen faith, and sweeten care,
5. Lord, we are few, but Thou art near; Nor short Thine arm, nor deaf Thine ear:

Wher-e'er they seek Thee, Thou art found, And ev-ery place is hallowed ground.
Such ev-er bring Thee where they come, And go-ing, take Thee to their home.
Here to our wait-ing hearts proclaim The sweetness of Thy saving name.
To teach our faint de-sires to rise, And bring all heaven be-fore our eyes.
O rend the heavens, come quickly down, And make a thousand hearts Thine own.

No. 192. The Christian Farewell.

1 Thy presence, everlasting God,
　Wide o'er all nature spreads abroad;
　Thy watchful eyes, which cannot sleep,
　In every place Thy children keep.

2 While near each other we remain,
　Thou dost our lives and souls sustain;
　When absent, Thou dost make us share
　Thy smiles, thy counsels, and Thy care.

3 To Thee we all our ways commit,
　And seek our comforts at Thy feet;
　Still on our souls vouchsafe to shine,
　And guard and guide us still as Thine.
　　　　　Rev. Philip Doddridge.

No. 193. With Tearful Eyes.

1 With tearful eyes I look around;
　Life seems a dark and stormy sea;
　Yet 'midst the gloom I hear a sound,
　A heavenly whisper, "Come to me!"

2 It tells me of a place of rest—
　It tells me where my soul may flee;
　Oh! to the weary, faint, oppressed,
　How sweet the bidding, "Come to me."

3 Come, for all else must fall and die,
　Earth is no resting-place for thee;
　Heavenward direct thy weeping eye;
　I am thy portion, "Come to me."

No. 194. He Wills.

1 He wills that I should holy be;
　That holiness I long to feel;
　That full divine conformity
　To all my Saviour's righteous will.

2 See, Lord, the travail of Thy soul
　Accomplished in the change of mine;
　And plunge me, every whit made whole,
　In all the depths of love divine.

3 On Thee, O God, my soul is stayed,
　And waits to prove Thine utmost will
　The promise by Thy mercy made,
　Thou canst, Thou wilt, in me fulfil.

No. 195. 'Tis by the Faith.

1 'Tis by the faith of joys to come,
　We walk thro' deserts dark as night;
　Till we arrive at heaven, our home,
　Faith is our guide, and faith our light.

2 The want of sight she well supplies;
　She makes the pearly gates appear;
　Far into distant worlds she pries,
　And brings eternal glories near.

3 Cheerful we tread the desert through,
　While faith inspires a heavenly ray;
　Though lions roar and tempests blow,
　And rocks and dangers fill the way.

No. 196. IN THE CROSS OF CHRIST. 8s & 7s.

Ithamar Conkey. (1815—1867.) 1851.

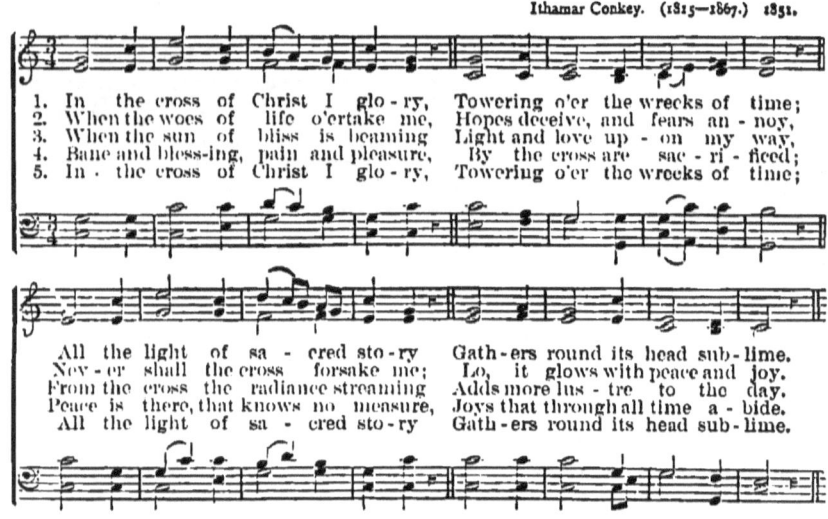

1. In the cross of Christ I glo-ry, Towering o'er the wrecks of time;
2. When the woes of life o'ertake me, Hopes deceive, and fears an-noy,
3. When the sun of bliss is beaming Light and love up-on my way,
4. Bane and bless-ing, pain and pleasure, By the cross are sac-ri-ficed;
5. In the cross of Christ I glo-ry, Towering o'er the wrecks of time;

All the light of sa-cred sto-ry Gath-ers round its head sub-lime.
Nev-er shall the cross forsake me; Lo, it glows with peace and joy.
From the cross the radiance streaming Adds more lus-tre to the day.
Peace is there, that knows no measure, Joys that through all time a-bide.
All the light of sa-cred sto-ry Gath-ers round its head sub-lime.

No. 197. Invocation.

1 Saviour! visit Thy plantation;
Grant us, Lord, a gracious rain;
All will come to desolation,
Unless Thou return again.

2 Keep no longer at a distance—
Shine upon us from on high,
Lest, for want of Thine assistance,
Every plant should droop and die.

3 Let our mutual love be fervent,
Make us prevalent in prayers;
Let each one, esteemed Thy servant,
Shun the world's enticing snares.

4 Break the tempter's fatal power;
Turn the stony heart to flesh;
And begin from this good hour,
To revive Thy work afresh.

No. 198. Before the Throne.

1 Hark the sound of holy voices,
Chanting at the crystal sea,
Hallelujah, Hallelujah,
Hallelujah! Lord, to Thee.

2 Multitude, which none can number,
Like the stars in glory stand,
Clothed in white apparel, holding
Palms of victory in their hand.

No. 199. Upon the Waters.

1 Cast thy bread upon the waters,
Thinking not 'tis thrown away;
God Himself saith, thou shalt gather
It again some future day.

2 Cast thy bread upon the waters;
Wildly though the billows roll,
They but aid thee as thou toilest
Truth to spread from pole to pole.

No. 200. Christian Children.

1 We are little Christian children;
We can run, and talk, and play;
The great God of earth and heaven
Made, and keeps us every day.

2 We are little Christian children;
Christ, the Son of God Most High,
With His precious blood redeemed us,
Dying that we might not die.

3 We are little Christian children;
God the Holy Ghost is here,
Dwelling in our hearts, to make us
Kind and holy, good and dear.

4 We are little Christian children,
Saved by Him who loved us most;
We believe in God Almighty,
Father, Son and Holy Ghost.

Mrs. Cecil Frances Alexander.

No. 201. WHERE IS THY REFUGE?

"What is a man profited, if he shall gain the whole world, and lose his own soul?"

FANNY J. CROSBY. S. J. VAIL.

1. Say, where is thy ref-uge, my broth-er, And what is thy pros-pect to - day?

Why toil for the wealth that will per - ish, The treasures that rust and de - cay?

O, think of thy soul, that for - ev - er Must live on e - ter - ni - ty's shore,

When thou in the dust art for - got - ten, When pleasure can charm thee no more.

CHORUS.

'Twill prof - it thee nothing, but fear-ful the cost, To gain the whole world, if thy

soul should be lost! To gain the whole world, if thy soul should be lost!

2 The Master is calling thee, brother,
In tones of compassion and love,
To feel that sweet rapture of pardon,
And lay up thy treasure above:
O, kneel at the cross where He suffered,
To ransom thy soul from the grave;
The arm of His mercy will hold thee,
The arm that is mighty to save.—*Cho.*

3 The summer is waning, my brother,
Repent, ere the season is past:
God's goodness to thee is extended,
As long as the day-beam shall last;
Then slight not the warning repeated
With all the bright moments that roll,
Nor say, when the harvest is ended,
That no one hath cared for thy soul. *Cho.*

By permission of Biglow & Main Co., owners of copyright.

No. 202.   O COULD I SPEAK.   C. P. M.

Arr. from Mozart by Lowell Mason. (1792—1872.) 1836.

1. O could I speak the matchless worth, O could I sound the glories forth,
2. I'd sing the precious blood He spilt, My ransom from the dreadful guilt
3. I'd sing the characters He bears, And all the forms of love He wears,
4. Well, the delightful day will come When my dear Lord will bring me home,

Which in my Saviour shine, I'd soar, and touch the heavenly strings, And vie with Gabriel
Of sin and wrath divine; I'd sing His glorious righteousness, In which all perfect,
Exalted on His throne; In loftiest songs of sweetest praise, I would to ever-
And I shall see His face; Then with my Saviour, Brother, Friend, A blest eterni-

while he sings In notes almost divine, In notes almost divine.
heavenly dress My soul shall ever shine, My soul shall ever shine.
lasting days Make all His glories known, Make all His glories known.
ty I'll spend, Triumphant in His grace, Triumphant in His grace.

No. 203. Verzage Nicht.

1 Fear not, O little flock, the foe
  Who madly seeks your overthrow,
    Dread not his rage and power:
  What though your courage sometimes faints,
  His seeming triumph o'er God's saints
    Lasts but a little hour.

2 As true as God's own word is true,
  Not earth nor hell with all their crew
    Against us shall prevail.
  A jest and byword are they grown:
  God is with us; we are his own;
    Our victory cannot fail.

3 Amen, Lord Jesus, grant our prayer!
  Great Captain, now Thine arm make bare;
    Fight for us once again!
  So shall Thy saints and martyrs raise
  A mighty chorus to Thy praise,
    World without end.
                        Gustavus Adolphus.

No. 204. Desiring to Love.

1 O love divine, how sweet thou art!
  When shall I find my willing heart
    All taken up by Thee?
  I thirst, and faint, and die to prove
  The greatness of redeeming love,
    The love of Christ to me.

2 Stronger His love than death or hell;
  Its riches are unsearchable;
    The first-born sons of light
  In vain desire its depths to see;
  They cannot reach the mystery,
    The length, and breadth, and height.

3 God only knows the love of God;
  O that it now were shed abroad
    In this poor, stony heart!
  For love I sigh, for love I pine;
  This only portion, Lord, be mine,
    Be mine this better part.
                        Rev. Charles Wesley.

No. 205. THE SOUL'S CRY ANSWERED. L. M.

"Come unto me." — Daniel Read.

1. Show pity, Lord! O Lord, forgive; Let a repenting rebel live; Are not Thy mercies large and free? May not a sinner trust in Thee?

2 My crimes are great, but don't surpass
The power and glory of Thy grace;
Great God! Thy nature hath no bound;
So let Thy pardoning love be found.

3 O wash my soul from every sin,
And make my guilty conscience clean;
Here on my heart the burden lies,
And past offences pain my eyes.

4 My lips with shame my sins confess,
Against Thy law, against Thy grace;
Lord, should Thy judgment grow severe,
I am condemned, but Thou art clear.

No. 206. The Sins of Men.

1 Arise, my tenderest thoughts, arise;
To torrents melt, my streaming eyes;
And thou, my heart, with anguish feel
Those evils which thou canst not heal.

2 See human nature sunk in shame;
See scandals poured on Jesus' name;
The Father wounded thro' the Son;
The world abused, the soul undone.

3 My God, I feel the mournful scene;
My spirit yearns o'er dying men;
And fain my pity would reclaim
And snatch the firebrands from the flame.

4 But feeble my compassion proves,
And can but weep where most it loves;
Thy own all-saving arm employ,
And turn these drops of grief to joy.
Rev. Philip Doddridge.

No. 207. Vision of Dry Bones.

1 Look down, O Lord, with pitying eye;
See Adam's race in ruin lie;
Sin spreads its trophies o'er the ground,
And scatters slaughtered heaps around.

2 And can these mouldering corpses live?
And can these perished bones revive?
That, mighty God, to Thee is known;
That wondrous work is all Thine own.

No. 208. Come, Sacred Spirit!

1 Come, Sacred Spirit, from above,
And fill the coldest heart with love;
Soften to flesh the rugged stone,
And let Thy god-like power be known.

2 Speak Thou, and from the haughtiest eyes
Shall floods of pious sorrow rise;
While all their glowing souls are borne
To seek that grace which now they scorn.

3 O let a holy flock await,
Numerous around Thy temple-gate,
Each pressing on with zeal to be
A living sacrifice to Thee.
Rev. Philip Doddridge.

No. 209. Hoping for a Revival.

1 While I to grief my soul gave way,
To see the work of God decline,
Methought I heard the Saviour say,
"Dismiss thy fears, the ark is Mine."

2 Though for a time I hide My face,
Rely upon My love and power;
Still wrestle at a throne of grace,
And wait for a reviving hour."
Rev. John Newton.

No. 210. NEW HAVEN. 6s & 4s.

RAY PALMER. *"Have faith in God."* Dr. T. HASTINGS.

1. My faith looks up to Thee, Thou Lamb of Cal-vary, Saviour di-vine! Now hear me while I pray, Take all my guilt a-way, O, let me from this day Be wholly Thine.

2 May Thy rich grace impart
Strength to my fainting heart,
My zeal inspire:
As Thou hast died for me,
O, may my love to Thee
Pure, warm, and changeless be—
A living fire.

3 While life's dark maze I tread,
And griefs around me spread,
Be Thou my guide;
Bid darkness turn to day;
Wipe sorrow's tears away,
Nor let me ever stray
From Thee aside.

No. 211. SAVIOUR, I LOOK TO THEE.

1 Saviour, I look to Thee,
Be not Thou far from me,
'Mid storms that lower:
On me Thy care bestow,
Thy loving kindness show,
Thine arms around me throw,
This trying hour.

2 Saviour, I look to Thee,
Feeble as infancy,
Gird up my heart:
Author of life and light,
Thou hast an arm of might,
Thine is the sovereign right,
Thy strength impart.

Thomas Hastings.

No. 212. SAFE FROM EVERY HARM. C. M.

HAVERGAL.

"Every day will I bless thee."

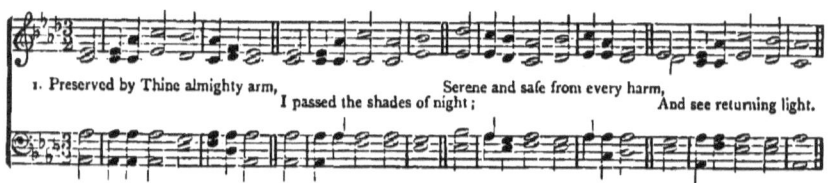

1. Preserved by Thine almighty arm, Serene and safe from every harm, I passed the shades of night; And see returning light.

2 While many spent the night in sighs,
And restless pains and woes,
In gentle sleep I closed my eyes,
And undisturbed repose.

3 Oh, let the same almighty care
My waking hours attend,
From every danger, every snare,
My heedless steps defend.

No. 213. RETREAT. L. M.

"Pray without ceasing." Dr. T. Hastings.

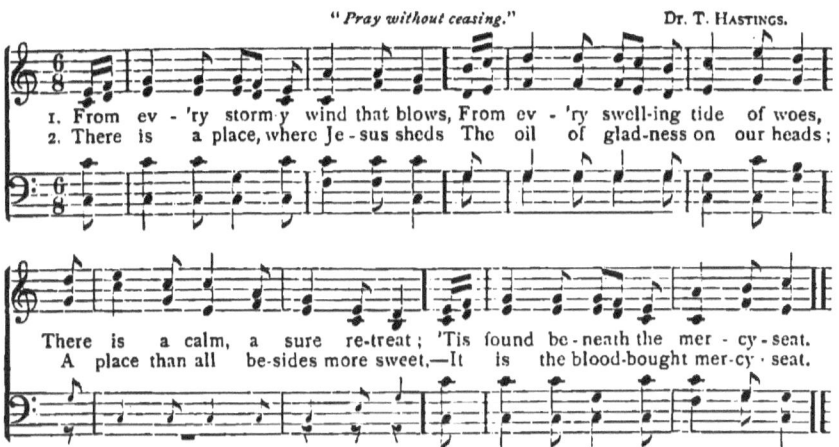

1. From ev-'ry storm-y wind that blows, From ev-'ry swell-ing tide of woes,
2. There is a place, where Je-sus sheds The oil of glad-ness on our heads;

There is a calm, a sure re-treat; 'Tis found be-neath the mer-cy-seat.
A place than all be-sides more sweet,—It is the blood-bought mer-cy-seat.

3 There is a scene, where spirits blend,
Where friend holds fellowship with friend;
Though sundered far, by faith they meet
Around one common mercy-seat.

4 There, there on eagles' wings we soar,
And sin and sense molest no more;
And heaven comes down our souls to greet,
While glory crowns the mercy-seat.
Hugh Stowell.

No. 214. Star of Bethlehem.

1 When marshaled on the nightly plain,
The glittering host bestud the sky,
One star alone of all the train
Can fix the sinner's wandering eye.

2 Hark, hark! to God the chorus breaks
From every host, from every gem;
But one alone the Saviour speaks,
It is the Star of Bethlehem.

3 Once on the raging seas I rode,
The storm was loud, the night was dark,
The ocean yawned, and rudely blowed
The wind that tossed my foundering bark.

4 Deep horror then my vitals froze;
Death-struck, I ceased the tide to stem:
When suddenly a star arose,
It was the Star of Bethlehem.

5 It was my guide, my light, my all,
It bade my dark forebodings cease;
And, through the storm and danger's thrall,
It led me to the port of peace.

6 Now safely moored, my perils o'er,
I'll sing, first in night's diadem,
For ever and for evermore,
The Star, the Star of Bethlehem.
Henry Kirke White.

No. 215. Quæ Stella Sole Pulchrior.

1 What star is this, with beams so bright,
Which shame the sun's less radiant light?
It shines to announce a new-born King,
Glad tidings of our God to bring.

2 'Tis now fulfilled what God decreed,
"From Jacob shall a star proceed:"
And lo, the Eastern sages stand,
To read in heaven the Lord's command.

3 O Jesus, while the star of grace
Invites us now to seek Thy face,
May we no more that grace repel,
Or quench that light which shines so well.
Prof. Charles Coffin.

No. 216. God's Unspeakable Glory.

1 Come, O my soul, in sacred lays
Attempt thy great Creator's praise:
But O, what tongue can speak His fame?
What mortal verse can reach the theme?

2 Enthroned amid the radiant spheres,
He glory like a garment wears,
To form a robe of light divine,
Ten thousand suns around Him shine.

No. 217.   AZMON. C.M.

From GLASER.

1. Come, let us join our cheerful songs With angels round the throne;
Ten thousand thousand were their tongues, And all their joys are one.

2 "Worthy the Lamb that died," they cry,
  "To be exalted thus:"
  "Worthy the Lamb," our lips reply,
  "For He was slain for us."

3 Jesus is worthy to receive
  Honor and power divine;
  And blessings, more than we can give,
  Be, Lord, forever Thine.

4 The whole creation join in one,
  To bless the sacred Name
  Of Him that sits upon the throne,
  And to adore the Lamb.—Wesley.

No. 218. Speak Gently.

1 Speak gently: it is better far
  To rule by love than fear;
  Speak gently: let no harsh word mar
  The good we may do here.

2 Speak gently to the little child:
  Its love be sure to gain;
  Teach it in accents soft and mild;
  It may not long remain.

No. 219. Christ a Pattern.

1 By cool Siloam's shady rill
  How sweet the lily grows!
  How sweet the breath beneath the hill
  Of Sharon's dewy rose!

2 Lo, such the child whose early feet
  The paths of peace have trod;
  Whose secret heart, with influence sweet,
  Is upward drawn to God.

No. 220. Shepherd of Israel.

1 Shepherd of Israel, from above
  Thy feeble flock behold;
  And never let us lose Thy love,
  Nor wander from Thy fold.

2 Thou wilt not cast Thy lambs away;
  Thy hand is ever near,
  To guide them lest they go astray,
  And keep them safe from fear.

No. 221. Hail, Sacred Truth.

1 Hail, sacred truth, whose piercing rays
  Dispel the shades of night;
  Diffusing, o'er the mental world,
  The healing beams of light.

2 Jesus, Thy word, with friendly aid,
  Restores our wandering feet;
  Converts the sorrows of the mind
  To joys divinely sweet.

No. 222. The Story Handed Down.

1 Let children hear the mighty deeds,
  Which God performed of old;
  Which in our younger years we saw,
  And which our fathers told.

2 He bids us make His glories known,
  His works of power and grace;
  And we'll convey His wonders down
  Through every rising race.

No. 223. Humble Service.

1 Scorn not the slightest word or deed,
  Nor deem it void of power;
  There's fruit in each wind-wafted seed,
  That waits its natal hour.

2 A whispered word may touch the heart,
  And call it back to life;
  A look of love bid sin depart,
  And still unholy strife.

No. 224. TRUST HIM ON THE FOAMY SEA.

"And there was a calm." PHILIP PHILLIPS.

1. Trust in God, for ev-ery bless-ing, Trust in God from day to day;
When the storm-y tem-pest rag-es, Go, by sim-ple faith, and pray.

2. God will nev-er fail His chil-dren, If His prom-ise they be-lieve;
In the pre-cious name of Je-sus All we ask, we shall re-ceive.

CHORUS.
Trust Him while He gives you breath, Trust Him in the vale of death,
Trust Him on the foam-y sea, Trust Him thro' e-ter-ni-ty.

3 Are the ties of earthly friendship
Crushed and broken, one by one?
Trust in God, and say, rejoicing,
Lord, Thy will, not mine, be done!—*Cho.*

4 Trust in God, the Rock of Ages,
Then thy feet shall stand secure;
Bear thy cross without repining,
Patient to the end endure.—*Cho.*

No. 225. DESIRED OF ALL NATIONS.

1 Come, Thou long-expected Jesus,
Born to set Thy people free;
From our fears and sins release us,
Let us find our rest in Thee.

2 Israel's Strength and Consolation,
Hope of all the earth Thou art;
Dear Desire of every nation,
Joy of every longing heart.

3 Born Thy people to deliver,
Born a Child, and yet a King,
Born to reign in us for ever,
Now Thy gracious kingdom bring.

4 By Thine own eternal Spirit,
Rule in all our hearts alone;
By Thine all-sufficient merit,
Raise us to Thy glorious throne.

Rev. Charles Wesley.

No. 226. HEAR MY CRY.
"*Hear my cry.*"
PHILIP PHILLIPS.

1. Son of David, hear my cry! Saviour, do not pass me by; Touch these eyelids veiled in night, Turn their darkness in-to light. Son of David, hear my cry! Saviour, do not pass me by.

2 Though the proud my voice would still,
They may chide me if they will,
Yet the more I'll pray for grace,
Only here shall be my place.
Son of David, hear my cry!
Saviour, do not pass me by.

3 Though despised by all but Thee,
Thou a blessing hast for me;
Faith and prayer can never fail,
Lord, with Thee I *must* prevail.
Son of David, hear my cry!
Saviour, do not pass me by.

4 Glorious vision! heavenly ray!
All my gloom has passed away;
Now my joyful eye doth see,
And my soul still clings to Thee;
Thine the glory evermore,
Mine to worship and adore.

No. 227. THE PILGRIM'S GUIDE.

1 GUIDE me, O thou great Jehovah!
Pilgrim through this barren land.
I am weak, but Thou art mighty,
Hold me with Thy powerful hand.
Bread of heaven, Bread of heaven,
Feed me till I want no more.

2 Open now the crystal fountain,
Whence the healing waters flow;
Let the fiery, cloudy pillar
Lead me all my journey through:
Strong Deliverer, Strong Deliverer,
Be Thou still my strength and shield.

3 When I tread the verge of Jordan,
Bid my anxious fears subside;
Bear me through the swelling current,
Land me safe on Canaan's side:
Songs of praises, Songs of praises,
I will ever give to Thee.—William Williams.

No. 228. LEBANON. S. M.
"*I am the good Shepherd.*"
J. ZUNDEL.

1. I was a wand'ring sheep, I did not love the fold; I did not love my Shepherd's voice, I would not be con-trolled; I loved a-far to roam. I was a wayward child, I did not love my home,

2 The Shepherd sought His sheep,
The Father sought His child;
They followed me o'er vale and hill,
O'er deserts waste and wild:
They found me nigh to death,
Famished, and faint, and lone;
They bound me with the bands of love,
They saved the wandering one.

3 Jesus my Shepherd is,
'Twas He that loved my soul,
'Twas He that washed me in His blood,
'Twas He that made me whole;
'Twas He that sought the lost,
That found the wandering sheep,
'Twas He that brought me to the fold,
'Tis He that still doth keep.—**Bonar.**

COME TO JESUS; HE WILL SAVE YOU NOW.

No. 229. *" Come unto Me and be ye saved."*

Words and Music by Rev. J. H. STOCKTON.

1. Come, ev - 'ry soul by sin op - press'd, There's mer - cy with the Lord;

And He will sure - ly give you rest, By trust - ing in His word.

CHORUS.

Come to Je - sus, come to Je - sus, Come to Je - sus now!

He will save you, He will save you, He will save you now.

2 Yes, Jesus is the Truth, the way
That leads you into rest;
Believe in Him without delay,
And you are fully blest.—*Chorus.*

3 Come, then, and join this holy band,
And on to glory go;
To dwell in that celestial land,
Where joys immortal flow.—*Chorus.*

No. 230. **"NINETY AND NINE."**

1 THERE were ninety and nine that safely lay
In the shelter of the fold,
But one was out on the hills away,
Far off from the gates of gold—
Away on the mountains wild and bare,
Away from the tender Shepherd's care.

2 " Lord, Thou hast here Thy ninety and nine:
Are they not enough for Thee?"
But the Shepherd made answer: " This of mine,
Has wandered away from me:
And although the road be rough and steep
I go to the desert to find my sheep,"

3 But none of the ransomed ever knew
How deep were the waters crossed ;
How dark the night the Lord passed thro'
Ere He found His sheep that was lost.
Out in the desert He heard its cry—
Sick and helpless, and ready to die.

4 But all thro' the mountains, thunder-riven,
And up from the rocky steep,
There rose a cry to the gate of heaven,
" Rejoice ! I have found my sheep !"
And the angels echoed around the throne,
" Rejoice, for the Lord brings back His own !"
Chaplaine.

No. 231. AWAKE, AND SING THE SONG. S. M.

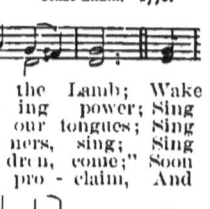
Isaac Smith. 1770.

1. A-wake, and sing the song Of Mo-ses and the Lamb; Wake ev-ery heart and ev-ery tongue, To praise the Sav-iour's name.
2. Sing of His dy-ing love; Sing of His ris-ing power; Sing how He in-ter-cedes a-bove For those whose sins He bore.
3. Sing till we feel our hearts As-cend-ing with our tongues; Sing till the love of sin de-parts, And grace in-spires our songs.
4. Sing on your heavenly way, Ye ransomed sin-ners, sing; Sing on, re-joic-ing ev-ery day In Christ the eter-nal King.
5. Soon shall ye hear Him say, "Ye bless-ed chil-dren, come;" Soon will He call you hence a-way, And take His wan-derers home.
6. There shall our rap-tured tongue His end-less praise pro-claim, And sweeter voi-ces swell the song Of Mo-ses and the Lamb.

No. 232. A Holy God Worshiped.

1 Exalt the Lord our God,
   And worship at His feet;
   His nature is all holiness,
   And mercy is His seat.

2 When Israel was His church,
   When Aaron was His priest,
   When Moses cried, and Samuel prayed,
   He gave His people rest.

3 Oft He forgave their sins,
   Nor would destroy their race;
   And oft He made His vengeance known
   When they abused His grace.

4 Exalt the Lord our God,
   Whose grace is still the same;
   Still He's a God of holiness,
   And jealous for His name.
   Rev. Isaac Watts.

No. 233. Invocation.

1 Come, Holy Spirit, come,
   With energy divine,
   And on this poor benighted soul,
   With beams of mercy shine.

2 From the celestial hills,
   Light, life and joy dispense;
   And may I daily, hourly feel
   Thy quickening influence.

3 O melt this frozen heart,
   This stubborn will subdue;
   Each evil passion overcome,
   And form me all anew.

4 The profit will be mine,
   But thine shall be the praise;
   Cheerful to Thee will I devote
   The remnant of my days.
   Rev. Benjamin Beddome.

No. 234. Prayer for the Spirit.

1 O for the happy hour
   When God will hear our cry,
   And send, with a reviving power,
   His Spirit from on high.

2 We meet, we sing, we pray,
   We listen to the word,
   In vain—we see no cheering ray,
   No cheering voice is heard.

3 While many crowd Thy house,
   How few, around Thy board.,
   Meet to record their solemn vows,
   And bless Thee as their Lord.

4 Thou, Thou alone canst give
   Thy gospel sure success,
   And bid the dying sinner live
   Anew in holiness.

5 Come, with Thy power divine,
   Spirit of life and love;
   Then shall our people all be Thine,
   Our church like that above.
   Rev. George Washington Bethune.

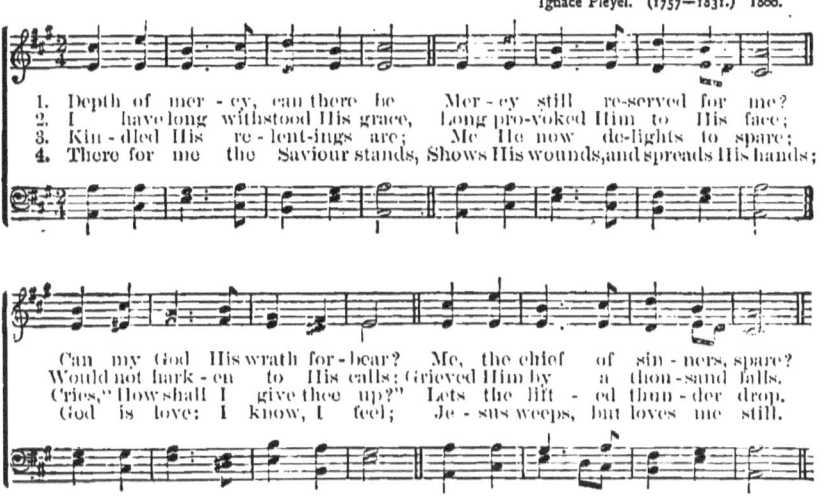

Ignace Pleyel. (1757—1831.) 1800.

1. Depth of mer - cy, can there be Mer - cy still re-served for me? Can my God His wrath for-bear? Me, the chief of sin - ners, spare?
2. I have long withstood His grace, Long pro-voked Him to His face; Would not hark - en to His calls; Grieved Him by a thou-sand falls.
3. Kin - dled His re - lent-ings are; Me He now de-lights to spare; Cries, "How shall I give thee up?" Lets the lift - ed thun - der drop.
4. There for me the Saviour stands, Shows His wounds, and spreads His hands; God is love: I know, I feel; Je - sus weeps, but loves me still.

No. 236. The Lord's Courts.

1 To Thy temple I repair;
Lord, I love to worship there;
When within the veil I meet
Christ before the mercy-seat.

2 While Thy glorious praise is sung,
Touch my lips, unloose my tongue,
That my joyful soul may bless
Thee, the Lord my righteousness.

3 While the prayers of saints ascend,
God of love, to mine attend;
Hear me, for Thy Spirit pleads,
Hear, for Jesus intercedes.

4 While Thy ministers proclaim
Peace and pardon in Thy name,
Through their voice, by faith, may I
Hear Thee speaking from the sky.

5 From Thy house when I return,
May my heart within me burn;
And at evening let me say,
"I have walked with God to-day."

James Montgomery.

No. 237. Redeeming Love.

1 Now begin the heavenly theme,
Sing aloud in Jesus' name;
Ye who Jesus' kindness prove,
Triumph in redeeming love.

2 Ye who see the Father's grace
Beaming in the Saviour's face,
As to Canaan on ye move,
Praise and bless redeeming love.

3 Mourning souls, dry up your tears;
Banish all your guilty fears;
See your guilt and curse remove,
Canceled by redeeming love.

4 Welcome, all by sin opprest,
Welcome to His sacred rest;
Nothing brought Him from above,
Nothing but redeeming love.

5 Hither, then, your music bring,
Strike aloud each joyful string;
Mortals, join the host above,
Join to praise redeeming love.

Rev. Martin Madan.

No. 238.   LORD, DISMISS US.   8s & 7s, 6 lines.

Jean Jacques Rousseau. (1712—1778.) 1750.

1. Lord, dismiss us with Thy blessing, Fill our hearts with joy and peace; Let us now, Thy love possessing, Triumph in redeeming grace: O refresh us, O refresh us, Traveling through this wilderness.
2. Thanks we give, and adoration, For Thy gospel's joyful sound: May the fruits of Thy salvation In our hearts and lives abound; May Thy presence, May Thy presence With us evermore be found.
3. So, whene'er the signal's given Us from earth to call away, Borne on angel wings to heaven, Glad the summons to obey, May we ever, May we ever Reign with Christ in endless day.

No. 239.   Prayer for Guidance.

1 Lead us, Heavenly Father, lead us
  O'er the world's tempestuous sea;
Guard us, guide us, keep us, feed us,
  For we have no help but Thee;
Yet possessing every blessing,
  If our God our Father be.

2 Saviour, breathe forgiveness o'er us;
  All our weakness Thou dost know;
Thou didst tread this earth before us;
  Thou didst feel its keenest woe;
Lone and dreary, faint and weary,
  Through the desert Thou didst go.

3 Spirit of our God, descending,
  Fill our hearts with heavenly joy,
Love with every passion blending,
  Pleasure that can never cloy;
Thus provided, pardoned, guided,
  Nothing can our peace destroy.
                    James Edmeston.

No. 240.   Ira Justa Conditoris.

1 He, Who once in righteous vengeance
  Whelmed the world beneath the flood,
Once again in mercy cleansed it
  With His own most precious blood;
Coming from His throne on high,
On the painful cross to die.

2 O the wisdom of the Eternal!
  O its depth, and height divine!
O the sweetness of that mercy
  Which in Jesus Christ did shine!
We were sinners doomed to die;
Jesus paid the penalty.

3 When before the Judge we tremble,
  Conscious of His broken laws,
May the blood of His atonement
  Cry aloud, and plead our cause;
Bid our guilty terrors cease,
Be our pardon and our peace.
            Translated by Rev. Edward Caswall.

No. 241. HOW FIRM A FOUNDATION. 11s.

John Reading. (1690—1766.) 1760.

1. How firm a foun-da-tion, ye saints of the Lord, Is laid for your faith in His excellent word! What more can He say than to you He hath said, You who un-to Je-sus for ref-uge have fled?
2. "Fear not, I am with thee,O be not dismayed, For I am thy God, and will still give thee aid; I'll strengthen thee,help thee,and cause thee to stand,Upheld by My righteous,om-nip - o - tent hand,
3. "When through the deep waters I call thee to go, The riv-ers of woe shall not thee o-verflow; For I will be with thee thy trouble to bless, And sanc-ti-fy to thee thy deepest distress,
4. "E'en down to old age, all My peo-ple shall prove My sovereign,e-ter-nal, un-changeable love; And when hoary hairs shall their temples adorn,Like lambs they shall still in My bosom be borne,
5. "The soul that on Je-sus hath leaned for repose I will not, I will not de-sert to his foes;That soul,though all hell should endeavor to shake, I'll never, no nev-er, no nev-er forsake,

Je-sus for ref-uge have fled? You who un-to Je-sus for ref-uge have fled?
righteous,om-nip - o - tent hand, Up-held by My righteous,om-nip - o - tent hand.
to thee thy deepest distress, And sanc-ti-fy to thee thy deepest dis-tress.
still in My bosom be borne, Like lambs they shall still in My bosom be borne.
nev-er, no nev-er forsake, I'll nev-er, no nev-er, no nev-er for-sake."

No. 242. Longing for Rest.

1 O had I, my Saviour, the wings of a dove,
  How soon would I soar to Thy presence above;
  How soon would I flee where the weary have rest,
  And hide all my cares in Thy sheltering breast.

2 I flutter, I struggle, I pant to get free;
  I feel me a captive while banished from Thee:
  A pilgrim and stranger, the desert I roam,
  And look on to heaven, and long to be home.

Rev. Henry Francis Lyte.

No. 243. Our Righteousness.

1 I once was a stranger to grace and to God,
  I knew not my danger, and felt not my load;
  Though friends spoke in rapture of Christ on the tree,
  Jehovah, my Saviour, seemed nothing to me.

2 When free grace awoke me by light from on high,
  Then legal fears shook me, I trembled to die;
  No refuge, no safety, in self could I see;
  Jehovah, Thou only my Saviour must be.

Rev. Robert Murray McCheyne.

No. 244. TAKE IT TO THE LORD IN PRAYER.

"*There is a Friend that sticketh closer than a brother.*" C. C. CONVERSE.

1. What a friend we have in Jesus, All our sins and griefs to bear;
What a priv-i-lege to car-ry Ev-'ry thing to God in prayer!
D.S. All be-cause we do not car-ry Ev-'ry thing to God in prayer!
Oh, what peace we of-ten for-feit, Oh, what needless pains we bear,—

2 Have we trials and temptations?
Is there trouble anywhere?
We should never be discouraged—
Take it to the Lord in prayer.
Can we find a friend so faithful,
Who will all our sorrows share?
Jesus knows our every weakness—
Take it to the Lord in prayer.

3 Are we weak and heavy laden,
Cumbered with a load of care?
Precious Saviour, still our refuge—
Take it to the Lord in prayer.
Do thy friends despise, forsake thee?
Take it to the Lord in prayer:
In His arms He'll take and shield thee.
Thou wilt find a solace there.

No. 245. Prayer for Union.

1 Hail, Thou God of grace and glory,
Who Thy name hast magnified,
By redemption's wondrous story,
By the Saviour crucified;
Thanks to Thee for every blessing,
Flowing from the Fount of love;
Thanks for present good unceasing,
And for hopes of bliss above.

2 Bind Thy people, Lord, in union,
With the sevenfold cord of love;
Breathe a spirit of communion
With the glorious hosts above;
Let Thy work be seen progressing;
Bow each heart, and bend each knee,
Till the world, Thy truth possessing,
Celebrates its jubilee.
Rev. Thomas William Aveling.

No. 246. A Lamp, and a Light.

1 How precious is the book divine
By inspiration given;
Bright as a lamp its doctrines shine,
To guide our souls to heaven.
Its light, descending from above,
Our gloomy world to cheer,
Displays a Saviour's boundless love,
And brings His glories near.

2 It shows to man his wandering ways,
And where his feet have trod;
And brings to view the matchless grace
Of a forgiving God.
Here the Redeemer's welcome voice,
Spreads heavenly peace around;
And life and everlasting joys
Attend the blissful sound.

No. 247. CHRISTMAS MORNING. C. M.

"*Glad tidings of great joy.*"

1. Angels rejoiced and sweetly sung,
   At our Redeemer's birth;
   Mortals, awake; let every tongue
   Proclaim His matchless worth.

2 Glory to God, who dwells on high,
   And sent His only Son
   To take a servant's form, and die
   For evils we had done.

3 Good-will to men; ye fallen race,
   Arise, and shout for joy;
   He comes, with rich, abounding grace
   To save, and not destroy.

4 Lord, send the gracious tidings forth,
   And fill the world with light,
   That Jew, and Gentile, through the earth,
   May know Thy saving might.
   Rev. William Hurn.

No. 248. Christmas Evening.

1 While shepherds watched their flocks by night,
   All seated on the ground,
   The angel of the Lord came down,
   And glory shone around.

2 "Fear not," said He—for mighty dread
   Had seized their trembling mind—
   "Glad tidings of great joy I bring
   To you and all mankind.

3 "All glory be to God on high,
   And to the earth be peace;
   Good-will henceforth from heaven to men,
   Begin, and never cease!"
   Nahum Tate.

No. 249. Majestic Sweetness.

1 No mortal can with Him compare,
   Among the sons of men;
   Fairer is He than all the fair
   That fill the heavenly train.

2 He saw me plunged in deep distress,
   He flew to my relief;
   For me He bore the shameful cross,
   And carried all my grief.

3 To Him I owe my life and breath,
   And all the joys I have;
   He makes me triumph over death,
   He saves me from the grave.
   S. Stennett.

No. 250. Breathing After Heaven.

1 Return, O God of love, return;
   Earth is a tiresome place:
   How long shall we, Thy children, mourn
   Our absence from Thy face?

2 Let heaven succeed our painful years,
   Let sin and sorrow cease;
   And, in proportion to our tears,
   So make our joys increase.

3 Thy wonders to Thy servants show,
   Make Thine own work complete;
   Then shall our souls Thy glory know,
   And own thy love was great.

4 Then shall we shine before Thy throne
   In all Thy beauty, Lord;
   And the poor service we have done
   Meet a divine reward.
   Rev. Isaac Watts.

No. 251. Riches of God's Word.

1 Father of mercies, in Thy word
   What endless glory shines!
   For ever be Thy name adored
   For these celestial lines.

2 Here may the wretched sons of want
   Exhaustless riches find;
   Riches above what earth can grant,
   And lasting as the mind.

3 Here the Redeemer's welcome voice
   Spreads heavenly peace around;
   And life and everlasting joys
   Attend the blissful sound.

No. 252. WE LONG TO MOVE IN THEE. C. M.

Thomas Augustine Arne. (1710—1778.) 1762.

1. We long to move and breathe in Thee, In-spired with Thine own breath;
2. Thy death to sin we die be-low, But we shall rise in love;
3. A-bove we shall Thy glo-ry share, As we, Thy cross have borne;
4. Thy crown of thorns is all our boast, While now we fall be-fore

To live Thy life, O Lord, and be Bap-tized in-to Thy death.
We here are plant-ed in Thy woe, But we shall bloom a-bove.
E'en we shall crowns of hon-or wear, When we the thorns have worn.
The Fa-ther, Son, and Ho-ly Ghost, And tremble, love, a-dore.

No. 253. Consolation in Sickness.

1 Sweet to look inward, and attend
   The whispers of His love;
Sweet to look upward to the place
   Where Jesus pleads above;

2 Sweet to reflect how grace divine
   My sins on Jesus laid;
Sweet to remember that His blood
   My debt of suffering paid.

3 If such the sweetness of the stream,
   What must the fountain be,
Where saints and angels draw their bliss
   Directly, Lord, from Thee!
                   A. M. Toplady.

No. 254. Praise to the Redeemer.

1 Plunged in a gulf of dark despair,
   We wretched sinners lay,
Without one cheerful beam of hope,
   Or spark of glimmering day.

2 With pitying eyes the Prince of grace
   Beheld our helpless grief;
He saw, and—O amazing love!—
   He ran to our relief.

3 Down from the shining seats above,
   With joyful haste He fled;
Entered the grave in mortal flesh,
   And dwelt among the dead.

4 O for this love, let rocks and hills
   Their lasting silence break;
And all harmonious human tongues
   The Saviour's praises speak.

5 Angels, assist our mighty joys,
   Strike all your harps of gold;
But when you raise your highest note,
   His love can ne'er be told.
                   Rev. Isaac Watts.

No. 255. The Way, the Truth, the Life.

1 Thou art the way: To Thee alone
   From sin and death we flee;
And he who would the Father seek,
   Must seek Him, Lord, by Thee.

2 Thou art the Truth: Thy word alone
   True wisdom can impart;
Thou only canst inform the mind,
   And purify the heart.

3 Thou art the Life: The rending tomb
   Proclaims Thy conquering arm,
And those who put their trust in Thee,
   Nor death, nor hell shall harm.

4 Thou art the Way, the Truth, the Life;
   Grant us that Way to know,
That Truth to keep, that Life to win,
   Whose joys eternal flow.
      Bishop George Washington Doane.

Xavier Schnyder von Wartensee. (1786—)

1. Come, said Jesus' sacred voice, Come, and make My paths your choice;
   I will guide you to your home, Weary pilgrim, hither come.
2. Thou who, houseless, sole, forlorn, Long hast borne the proud world's scorn,
   Long hast roamed the barren waste, Weary pilgrim, hither haste.
3. Ye who, tossed on beds of pain, Seek for ease, but seek in vain;
   Ye, by fiercer anguish torn, In remorse for guilt who mourn.
4. Hither come, for here is found Balm that flows for every wound,
   Peace that ever shall endure, Rest eternal, sacred, sure.

No. 257. Love's Sweet Lesson.

1 Saviour, teach me, day by day,
Love's sweet lesson to obey;
Sweeter lesson cannot be,
Loving Him who first loved me.

2 Teach me all Thy steps to trace,
Strong to follow in Thy grace;
Learning how to love from Thee,
Loving him who first loved me.

No. 258. Cast Thy Burden.

1 Cast thy burden upon the Lord,
Only lean upon His word;
Thou shalt soon have cause to bless
His eternal faithfulness.

2 Ever in the raging storm,
Thou shalt see His cheering form,
Hear His pledge of coming aid:
"It is I, be not afraid."

3 Cast thy burden at His feet;
Linger at His mercy-seat:
He will lead thee by the hand
Gently to the better land.
Rev. Rowland Hill.

No. 259. The Penitent Pardoned.

1 Sovereign Ruler, Lord of all,
Prostrate at Thy feet I fall;
Hear, O hear my ardent cry,
Frown not, lest I faint and die.

2 Justly might Thy vengeful dart
Pierce this bleeding, broken heart;
Justly might Thy kindled ire
Blast me in eternal fire.

3 But with Thee there's mercy found,
Balm to heal my every wound:
Thou canst soothe the troubled breast,
Give the weary wanderer rest.
Rev. Thos. Raffles.

No. 260. Rest in Christ.

1 Jesus, full of truth and love,
We Thy kindest word obey:
Faithful let Thy mercies prove,
Take our load of guilt away.

2 Burdened with a world of grief,
Burdened with our sinful load,
Burdened with this unbelief,
Burdened with the wrath of God;

3 Lo, we come to Thee for ease,
True and gracious as Thou art;
Now our groaning soul release,
Write forgiveness on our heart.
Rev. Charles Wesley.

Dr. L. Mason.

"Morning, noon, and night I will praise Thee."

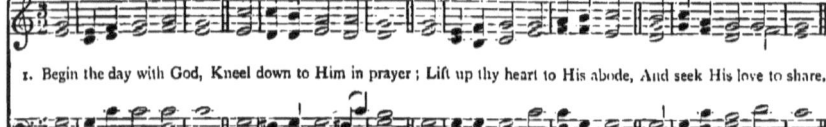

1. Begin the day with God, Kneel down to Him in prayer; Lift up thy heart to His abode, And seek His love to share.

2 Open the Book of God,
  And read a portion there;
That it may hallow all thy thoughts,
  And sweeten all thy care.

3 Go through the day with God,
  Whate'er thy work may be;
Where'er thou art—at home, abroad,
  He still is near to thee.

4 Conclude the day with God;
  Thy sins to Him confess;
Trust in the Lord's atoning blood,
  And plead His righteousness.
  Bennett.

No. 262. New Year's Morning.

1 A few more struggles here,
  A few more partings o'er,
A few more toils, a few more tears,
  And we shall weep no more.

2 A few more Sabbaths here
  Shall cheer us on our way,
And we shall reach the endless rest,
  Th' eternal Sabbath day.

3 Then, O my Lord, prepare
  My soul for that glad day;
O! wash me in Thy precious blood,
  And take my sins away.
  Horatius Bonar.

No. 263. New Year's Evening.

1 "For ever with the Lord!"
  Amen! so let it be;
Life from the dead is in that word;
  'Tis immortality.

2 Here, in the body pent,
  Absent from Him I roam,
Yet nightly pitch my moving tent
  A day's march nearer home.

3 Knowing as I am known,
  How shall I love that word,
And oft repeat before the throne,
  "For ever with the Lord!"
  James Montgomery.

No. 264. The Day is Past.

1 The day is past and gone,
  The evening shades appear,
O may we all remember well,
  The night of death draws near.

2 Lord, keep us safe this night,
  Secure from all our fears;
May angels guard us while we sleep,
  Till morning light appears.

3 And when our days are past,
  And we from time remove,
Lord, may we in Thy bosom rest,
  The bosom of Thy love.
  Leland.

No. 265. Watching Unto Prayer.

1 Jesus, my strength, my hope,
  On Thee I cast my care,
With humble confidence look up,
  And know Thou hears't my prayer.

2 Give me on Thee to wait,
  Till I can all things do;
On Thee, Almighty to create,
  Almighty to renew.

3 I want a sober mind,
  A self-renouncing will,
That tramples down, and casts behind
  The baits of pleasing ill;

4 A soul inured to pain,
  To hardship, grief and loss,
Bold to take up, firm to sustain
  That consecrated cross.

5 I want a godly fear,
  A quick-discerning eye,
That looks to Thee when sin is near,
  And sees the tempter fly;

6 A spirit still prepared,
  And armed with jealous care,
For ever standing on its guard,
  And watching unto prayer.
  Rev. Charles Wesley.

No. 266. ALL GOODNESS FLOWS. C. M.

REV. THOMAS HAWEIS.   HUGH WILSON. 1768.

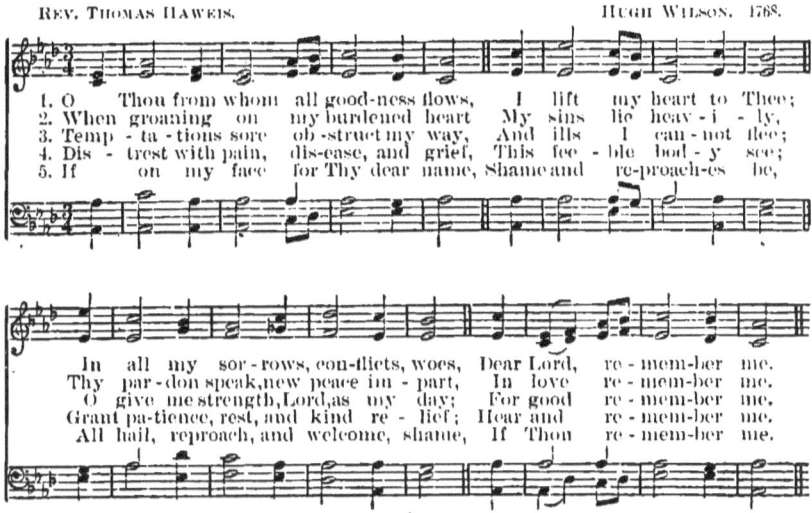

1. O Thou from whom all good-ness flows, I lift my heart to Thee;
2. When groaning on my burdened heart My sins lie heav-i-ly,
3. Temp-ta-tions sore ob-struct my way, And ills I can-not flee;
4. Dis-trest with pain, dis-ease, and grief, This fee-ble bod-y see;
5. If on my face for Thy dear name, Shame and re-proach-es be,

In all my sor-rows, con-flicts, woes, Dear Lord, re-mem-ber me.
Thy par-don speak, new peace im-part, In love re-mem-ber me.
O give me strength, Lord, as my day; For good re-mem-ber me.
Grant pa-tience, rest, and kind re-lief; Hear and re-mem-ber me.
All hail, reproach, and welcome, shame, If Thou re-mem-ber me.

No. 267. The Inner Calm.

1 Calm me, my God, and keep me calm,
 Soft resting on Thy breast;
Soothe me with holy hymn and psalm,
 And bid my spirit rest.

2 Calm me, my God, and keep me calm;
 Let Thine outstretched wing
Be like the shade of Elim's palm,
 Beside her desert spring.

3 Yes, keep me calm, though loud and rude
 The sounds my ear that greet;
Calm in the closet's solitude,
 Calm in the bustling street;

4 Calm in the hour of buoyant health,
 Calm in my hour of pain;
Calm in my poverty or wealth,
 Calm in my loss or gain.

No. 268. Lamp of Our Feet.

1 Lamp of our feet, whereby we trace
 Our path when wont to stray;
Stream from the Fount of heavenly grace,
 Brook by the traveler's way;

2 Bread of our souls, whereon we feed,
 True manna from on high;
Our guide and chart, wherein we read
 Of realms beyond the sky;

3 Word of the Everlasting God,
 Will of His glorious Son;
Without Thee how could earth be trod,
 Or heaven itself be won?

4 Lord, grant us all aright to learn
 The wisdom it imparts;
And to its heavenly teaching turn,
 With simple, child-like hearts.
   Bernard Barton.

No. 269. For Ever Here.

1 For ever here my rest shall be,
 Close to Thy bleeding side,
This all my hope, and all my plea,
 For me the Saviour died.

2 My dying Saviour, and my God,
 Fountain for guilt and sin,
Sprinkle me ever with Thy blood,
 And cleanse and keep me clean.

3 Wash me, and make me thus Thine own;
 Wash me, and mine Thou art;
Wash me, but not my feet alone,
 My hands, my head, my heart.
   C. Wesley.

No. 270. Israel's Gentle Shepherd.

1 See Israel's gentle Shepherd stand,
 With all-engaging charms;
Hark, how He calls the tender lambs,
 And folds them in His arms.

2 Permit them to approach, He cries,
 Nor scorn their humble name;
For 'twas to bless such souls as these
 The Lord of angels came.

3 We bring them, Lord, in thankful hands,
 And yield them up to Thee;
Joyful that we ourselves are Thine,
 Thine let our offspring be.

No. 271. AWAKE, MY SOUL. L. M.

Christian Lyre. 1830.

1. Awake, my soul, to joyful lays, And sing thy great Redeemer's praise; He justly claims a song from me,
2. He saw me ru-ined in the fall, Yet loved me notwithstanding all, And saved me from my lost estate,
3. Thro' mighty hosts of cruel foes, Where earth and hell my way oppose, He safely leads my soul along,

His loving-kindness is so free; Loving-kindness, Loving-kindness, His loving-kindness is so free.
His loving-kindness is so great; Loving-kindness, Loving-kindness, His loving-kindness is so great.
His loving-kindness is so strong; Loving-kindness, Loving-kindness, His loving-kindness is so strong.

No. 272. The Holy Spirit.

1 Come, Holy Ghost, all quickening fire,
  Come, and in me delight to rest;
  Drawn by the lure of strong desire,
  O come, and consecrate my breast;
  The temple of my soul prepare,
  And fix Thy sacred presence there.

2 My peace, my life, my comfort now,
  My treasure, and my all Thou art;
  True Witness of my sonship Thou,
  Engraving pardon on my heart;
  Seal of my sins in Christ forgiven,
  Earnest of love, and pledge of heaven.

3 Come, then, my God, mark out Thine heir,
  Of heaven a larger earnest give,
  With clearer light Thy witness bear;
  More sensibly within me live;
  Let all my powers Thy entrance feel,
  And deeper stamp Thyself the Seal.
    Rev. Charles Wesley.

No. 273. Veni Creator Spiritus.

1 Come, Holy Ghost, our souls inspire,
  And lighten with celestial fire;
  Thou the anointing Spirit art,
  Who dost Thy seven-fold gifts impart:
  Thy blessed unction from above
  Is comfort, life, and fire of love.

2 Enable with perpetual light
  The dullness of our blinded sight;
  Anoint and cheer our soiled face
  With the abundance of Thy grace;
  Keep far our foes, give peace at home;
  Where Thou art guide, no ill can come.

3 Teach us to know the Father, Son,
  And Thee, of both, to be but one;
  That through the ages all along,
  This still may be our endless song:
  All praise, with all the heavenly host,
  To Father, Son, and Holy Ghost!
    Translated by Bishop John Cosin.

No. 274. Groaning for the Spirit.

1 When shall I hear the inward voice,
  Which only faithful souls can hear?
  Pardon, and peace, and heavenly joys
  Attend the promised Comforter:
  He comes, and righteousness divine,
  And Christ, and all with Christ, is mine.

2 O that the Comforter would come,
  Nor visit as a transient guest;
  But fix in me His constant home,
  And keep possession of my breast,
  And make my soul His loved abode,
  The temple of indwelling God.

3 Come, Holy Ghost, my heart inspire;
  Attest that I am born again;
  Come, and baptize me now with fire,
  Or all Thy former gifts are vain.
  I cannot rest in sins forgiven;
  Where is the earnest of my heaven?

4 Where the indubitable seal,
  That ascertains the kingdom mine?
  The powerful stamp I long to feel,
  The signature of love divine:
  O shed it in my heart abroad,
  Fullness of love, of heaven, of God!
    Rev. Charles Wesley.

No. 275. VANISHING JOYS. 8s & 7s.

"Blessed are the dead that die in the Lord." I. B. WOODBURY.

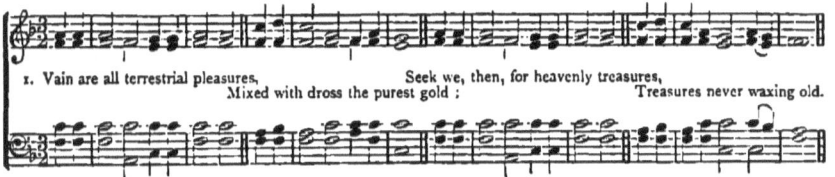

1. Vain are all terrestrial pleasures, Mixed with dross the purest gold; Seek we, then, for heavenly treasures, Treasures never waxing old.

2 Earthly joys can never please us;
  Here would we renounce them all;
  Seek our only rest in Jesus,
   Him our Lord and Master call.

3 Faith, our languid spirits cheering,
   Points to brighter worlds above,
   Bids us look for His appearing,
   Bids us triumph in His love.

4 Thus the Christian life adorning,
   Never need we be afraid,
   Should He come at night or morning,
   Early dawn, or evening shade.

No. 276. We Shall Meet and Rest.

1 Where the faded flow'r shall freshen—
   Freshen, never more to fade;
   Where the shaded sky shall brighten—
   Brighten, never more to shade;

2 Where the sunblaze never scorches,
   Where the starbeams cease to chill;
   Where no tempest stirs the echoes
   Of the wood, or wave, or hill;

3 Where the morn shall wake in gladness,
   And the noon the joy prolong;
   Where the daylight dies in fragrance,
   'Mid the burst of holy song.
   Rev. Dr. H. Bonar.

No. 277. Mercy.

1 "Mercy, O Thou Son of David!"
   Thus blind Bartimeus prayed;
   "Others by Thy word are saved,
   Now to me afford Thine aid."

2 Many for his crying chid him,
   But he called the louder still;
   Till the gracious Saviour bid him
   Come, and ask Me what you will.

No. 278. Thy Will be Done.

1 Jesus, while our hearts are bleeding
   O'er the spoils that death has won,
   We would, at this solemn meeting,
   Calmly say, Thy will be done.

2 Though cast down, we're not forsaken,
   Though afflicted, not alone;
   Thou didst give, and Thou hast taken;
   Blessed Lord, Thy will be done.

3 By Thy hands the boon was given;
   Thou hast taken but Thine own;
   Lord of earth, and God of heaven,
   Evermore, Thy will be done.

No. 279. Life's Raging Billow.

1 Tossed upon life's raging billow,
   Sweet it is, O Lord, to know,
   Thou didst press a sailor's pillow,
   And canst feel a sailor's woe.

2 Never slumb'ring, never sleeping,
   Tho' the night be dark and drear,
   Thou the faithful watch are keeping;
   "All, all's well," Thy constant cheer.

3 And though loud the wind is howling,
   Fierce though flash the lightnings red!
   Darkly though the storm-cloud's scowling
   O'er the sailor's anxious head:

4 Thou canst calm the raging ocean,
   All its noise and tumult still;
   Hush the tempest's wild commotion
   At the bidding of Thy will.

5 Thus my heart the hope will cherish
   While to Thee I lift mine eye,
   Thou wilt save me ere I perish,
   Thou wilt hear the sailor's cry.

6 And though mast and sail be riven,
   Life's short voyage will soon be o'er;
   Safely moored in heaven's wide haven,
   Storm and tempest vex no more.

No. 280. BEHOLD, A STRANGER. L. M.

William Batchelder Bradbury. (1816—1868.) 1844.

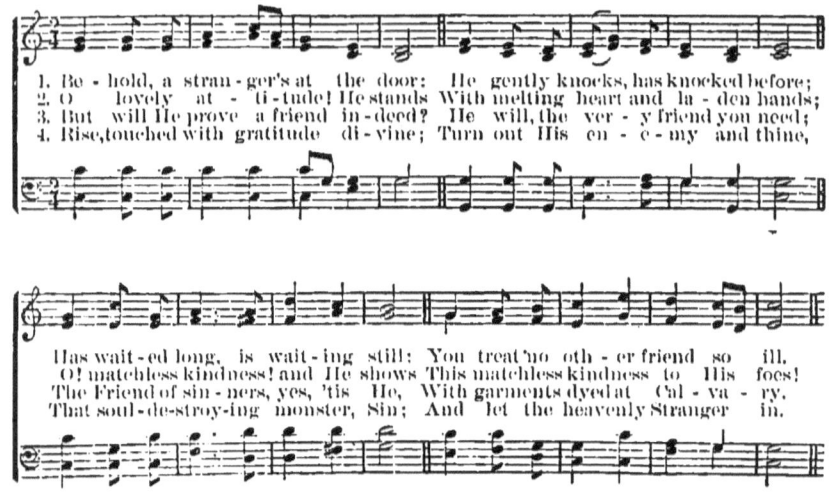

1. Be-hold, a stran-ger's at the door: He gently knocks, has knocked before;
2. O lovely at-ti-tude! He stands With melting heart and la-den hands;
3. But will He prove a friend in-deed? He will, the ver-y friend you need;
4. Rise, touched with gratitude di-vine; Turn out His en-e-my and thine,

Has wait-ed long, is wait-ing still; You treat no oth-er friend so ill.
O! matchless kindness! and He shows This matchless kindness to His foes!
The Friend of sin-ners, yes, 'tis He, With garments dyed at Cal-va-ry.
That soul-de-stroy-ing monster, Sin; And let the heavenly Stranger in.

No. 281. Slavery and Death.

1 Slavery and death the cup contains;
  Dash to the earth the poisoned bowl;
Softer than silk are iron chains
  Compared with those that chafe the soul.

2 Spare, Lord, the thoughtless, guide the blind,
  Till man no more shall deem it just
To live by forging chains to bind
  His weaker brother in the dust.

No. 282. With Christ in Glory.

1 O for a sweet, inspiring ray,
  To animate our feeble strains,
From the bright realms of endless day,
  The blissful realms, where Jesus reigns.

2 There, low before His glorious throne,
  Adoring saints and angels fall;
And with delightful worship own
  His smile their bliss, their heaven, their all.

3 Immortal glories crown His head,
  While tuneful hallelujahs rise,
And love, and joy, and triumph spread
  Through all th' assemblies of the skies.

4 He smiles, and seraphs tune their songs
  To boundless rapture while they gaze;
Ten thousand thousand joyful tongues
  Resound His everlasting praise.

5 There, all the favorites of the Lamb
  Shall join at last the heavenly choir:
O may the joy-inspiring theme
  Awake our faith and warm desire.

6 Dear Saviour, let Thy Spirit seal
  Our interest in that blissful place;
Till death remove this mortal veil,
  And we behold Thy lovely face.
    Miss Anne Steele.

No. 283. O Spirit.

1 O Spirit of the living God,
  In all Thy plentitude of grace,
Where'er the foot of man hath trod,
  Descend on our apostate race.

2 Give tongues of fire, and hearts of love,
  To preach the reconciling word;
Give power and unction from above,
  Whene'er the joyful sound is heard.

3 Be darkness, at Thy coming, light,
  Confusion, order in Thy path;
Souls without strength inspire with might;
  Bid mercy triumph over wrath.

4 Baptize the nations; far and nigh
  The triumphs of the cross record;
The name of Jesus glorify,
  Till every kindred call Him Lord.
    James Montgomery.

R. SIMPSON.

"*Lead Thou me on.*"

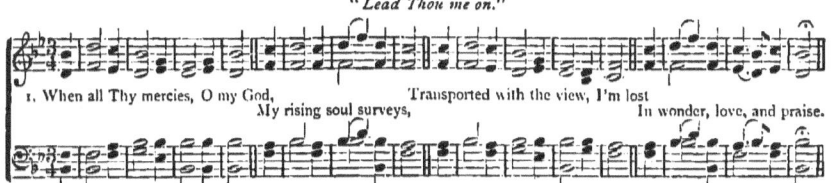

1. When all Thy mercies, O my God,
My rising soul surveys,
Transported with the view, I'm lost
In wonder, love, and praise.

2 Ten thousand thousand precious gifts,
My daily thanks employ,
Nor is the least a cheerful heart,
That tastes those gifts with joy.

3 Through every period of my life,
Thy goodness I'll pursue,
And after death in distant worlds
The glorious theme renew.

4 Through all eternity, to Thee,
A joyful song I'll raise,
For, oh! eternity's too short
To utter all Thy praise.
Addison.

No. 285. Awake, My Soul.

1 Awake, my soul, stretch every nerve,
And press with vigor on ;
A heavenly race demands thy zeal,
And an immortal crown.

2 A cloud of witnesses around
Hold thee in full survey ;
Forget the steps already trod,
And onward urge thy way.

3 Blest Saviour, introduced by Thee,
Have I my race begun ;
And, crowned with victory, at Thy feet
I'll lay my honors down.
Philip Doddridge.

No. 286. Prayer for Pity.

1 To Thee, my God, whose presence fills
The earth, and seas, and skies,
To Thee, whose name, whose heart is Love,
With all my powers I rise.

2 Troubles in long succession roll ;
Wave rushes upon wave ;
Pity, O pity my distress ;
Thy child, Thy suppliant save.

3 O bid the roaring tempest cease ;
Or give me strength to bear
Whate'er Thy holy will appoints,
And save me from despair.

4 To Thee, my God, alone I look,
On Thee alone confide ;
Thou never hast deceived the soul
That on Thy grace relied.

5 Though oft Thy ways are rapt in clouds
Mysterious and unknown,
Truth, Righteousness and Mercy stand
The pillars of Thy throne.
Rev. Thomas Gibbons.

No. 287. Grateful Thanks.

1 Now, from the altar of our hearts,
Let grateful thanks arise ;
Assist us, Lord, to offer up
Our evening's sacrifice.

2 Awake! our love, awake! our joy :
Awake! our heart and tongue ;
Sleep not when mercies loudly call :
Break forth into a song.

3 This day God was our sun and shield,
Our Keeper and our guide ;
His care was on our weakness shown,
His mercies multiplied.
Mason.

No. 288. Returning to God.

1 O Thou, whose tender mercy hears
Contrition's humble sigh,
Whose hand indulgent wipes the tears
From sorrow's weeping eye ;

2 See, low before Thy throne of grace,
A wretched wanderer mourn ;
Hast Thou not bid me seek Thy face?
Hast Thou not said, return ?

3 And shall my guilty fears prevail
To drive me from Thy feet?
O let not this dear refuge fail,
This only safe retreat !

4 O shine on this benighted heart,
With beams of mercy shine !
And let Thy healing voice impart
A taste of joys divine.

5 Thy presence only can bestow
Delights which never cloy :
Be this my solace here below,
And my eternal joy !
Miss Anne Steele.

No. 289. HARK, MY SOUL. 7s.

Rev. Cæsar Henri Abraham Malan. (1787–1864.) 1830.

1. Hark, my soul, it is the Lord; 'Tis thy Saviour, hear His word; Jesus speaks, and
2. "I delivered thee, when bound, And, when wounded, healed thy wound; Sought thee wandering,
3. "Can a woman's tender care Cease towards the child she bear? Yes, she may for-
4. "Mine is an unchanging love, Higher than the heights above, Deeper than the
5. "Thou shalt see My glory soon, When the work of grace is done; Partner of My
6. Lord, it is my chief complaint, That my love is weak and faint; Yet I love Thee,

speaks to thee; "Say, poor sinner, lovest thou Me? Say, poor sinner, lovest thou Me?
set thee right, Turned thy darkness in-to light, Turned thy darkness in-to light.
get-ful be, Yet will I remember thee, Yet will I remember thee.
depths beneath, Free and faithful, strong as death, Free and faithful, strong as death.
throne shall be, Say, poor sinner, lovest thou Me? Say, poor sinner, lovest thou Me?"
and a-dore; O for grace to love Thee more, O for grace to love Thee more.

No. 290. Tell Us of the Night.

1 Watchman! tell us of the night,
What its signs of promise are.
Trav'ler o'er yon mountain's height
See that glory-beaming star!

2 Watchman! does its beauteous ray
Aught of joy or hope foretell?
Trav'ler! yes; it brings the day—
Promised day of Israel.

3 Watchman! tell us of the night;
Higher yet that star ascends.
Trav'ler! blessedness and light,
Peace and truth, its course portends.

4 Watchman! will its beams alone
Gild the spot that gave them birth?
Trav'ler! ages are its own;
See, it bursts o'er all the earth!

5 Watchman! tell us of the night,
For the morning seems to dawn.
Trav'ler! darkness takes its flight,
Doubt and terror are withdrawn.

6 Watchman! let thy wanderings cease;
Hie thee to thy quiet home!
Trav'ler! lo! the Prince of Peace,
Lo! the Son of God is come!
J. Browning.

No. 291. Ask What I Shall Give.

1 Come, my soul, thy suit prepare,
Jesus loves to answer prayer;
He Himself has bid thee pray,
Therefore will not say thee nay.

2 Thou art coming to a King,
Large petitions with thee bring;
For His grace and power are such,
None can ever ask too much.

3 With my burden I begin,
Lord, remove this load of sin;
Let Thy blood, for sinners spilt,
Set my conscience free from guilt.
Rev. John Newton.

No. 292. He is Risen.

1 "Christ, the Lord, is risen to-day,"
Sons of men and angels say.
Raise your joys and triumphs high;
Sing, ye heavens; and earth, reply.

2 Love's redeeming work is done,
Fought the fight, the battle won.
Lo, our Sun's eclipse is o'er;
Lo, He sets in blood no more.

3 Vain the stone, the watch, the seal;
Christ has burst the gates of hell;
Death in vain forbids His rise;
Christ has opened paradise.

No. 293. HARK! WHAT MEAN THOSE VOICES? 8s & 7s.

Carl Maria von Weber. (1786—1826.)

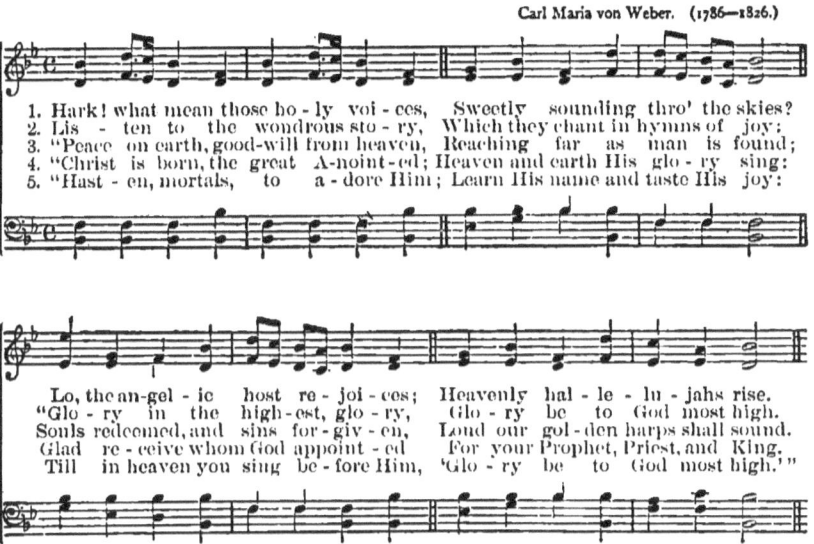

1. Hark! what mean those ho-ly voi-ces, Sweetly sounding thro' the skies?
2. Lis - ten to the wondrous sto - ry, Which they chant in hymns of joy;
3. "Peace on earth, good-will from heaven, Reaching far as man is found;
4. "Christ is born, the great A-noint-ed; Heaven and earth His glo - ry sing:
5. "Hast - en, mortals, to a - dore Him; Learn His name and taste His joy:

Lo, the an-gel - ic host re - joi - ces; Heavenly hal - le - lu - jahs rise.
"Glo - ry in the high-est, glo - ry, Glo - ry be to God most high.
Souls redeemed, and sins for-giv - en, Loud our gol - den harps shall sound.
Glad re - ceive whom God appoint - ed For your Prophet, Priest, and King.
Till in heaven you sing be - fore Him, 'Glo - ry be to God most high.'"

No. 294. God is Love.

1 God is love; His mercy brightens
   All the path in which we rove;
 Bliss He wakes, and woe He lightens,
   God is wisdom, God is love.

2 Time and change are busy ever;
   Man decays, and ages move;
 But His mercy waneth never;
   God is wisdom, God is love.

3 E'en the hour that darkest seemeth
   Will His changeless goodness prove;
 From the gloom His brightness stream-
     eth,
   God is wisdom, God is love.

4 He with earthly care entwineth
   Hope and comfort from above;
 Everywhere His glory shineth;
   God is wisdom, God is love.

No. 295. Christ Praised.

1 Brightness of the Father's glory,
   Shall Thy praise unuttered lie?
 Fly, my tongue, such guilty silence,
   Sing the Lord who came to die.

2 Did archangels sing Thy coming?
   Did the shepherds learn their lays?
 Shame would cover me ungrateful,
   Should my tongue refuse to praise.

3 From the highest throne of glory,
   To the cross of deepest woe—
 All to ransom guilty captives;
   Flow, my praise, for ever flow.

4 Go, return, immortal Saviour,
   Leave Thy footstool, take Thy throne;
 Thence return and reign for ever;
   Be the Kingdom all Thine own.
                    Rev. Robert Robinson.

No. 296. The Call for Reapers.

1 Far and near the fields are teeming
   With the waves of ripened grain;
 Far and near their gold is gleaming,
   O'er the sunny slope and plain.

Cho.—Lord of Harvest, send forth reapers!
   Hear us, Lord, to thee we cry;
 Send them now the sheaves to gather,
   Ere the harvest time pass by.

2 Send them forth with morn's first beam-
     ing,
   Send them in the noontide's glare;
 When the sun's last rays are gleaming,
   Bid them gather everywhere.—Cho.

3 O thou, whom thy Lord is sending,
   Gather now the sheaves of gold,
 Heavenward then at evening wending,
   Thou shalt come with joy untold.—Cho.

No. 297.   JUST AS I AM. L. M.

William Batchelder Bradbury. (1816—1868.) 1849.

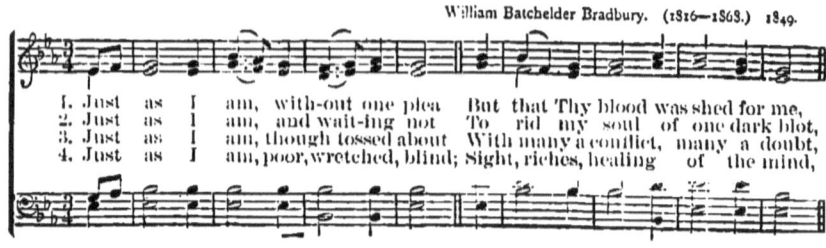

1. Just as I am, without one plea But that Thy blood was shed for me,
2. Just as I am, and waiting not To rid my soul of one dark blot,
3. Just as I am, though tossed about With many a conflict, many a doubt,
4. Just as I am, poor, wretched, blind; Sight, riches, healing of the mind,

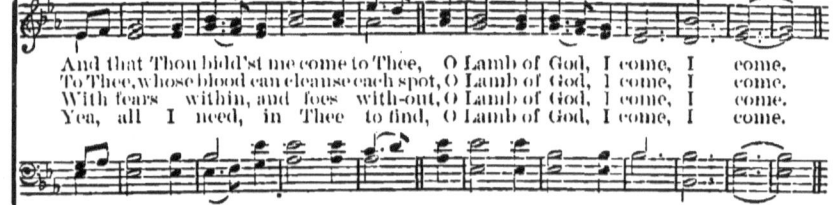

And that Thou bidd'st me come to Thee, O Lamb of God, I come, I come.
To Thee, whose blood can cleanse each spot, O Lamb of God, I come, I come.
With fears within, and foes without, O Lamb of God, I come, I come.
Yea, all I need, in Thee to find, O Lamb of God, I come, I come.

No. 298. He Leadeth Me.

1 He leadeth me! oh! blessed thought,
  Oh! words with heav'nly comfort fraught;
  Whate'er I do, where'er I be,
  Still 'tis God's hand that leadeth me.

Cho.—He leadeth me! He leadeth me!
  By His own hand He leadeth me;
  His faithful follower I would be,
  For by His hand He leadeth me.

2 Sometimes 'mid scenes of deepest gloom,
  Sometimes where Eden's bowers bloom,
  By waters still, o'er troubled sea—
  Still 'tis His hand that leadeth me.

3 Lord, I would clasp Thy hand in mine,
  Nor ever murmur nor repine—
  Content, whatever lot I see,
  Since 'tis my God that leadeth me.

4 And when my task on earth is done,
  When, by Thy grace the victory's won,
  E'en death's cold wave I will not flee,
  Since God through Jordan leadeth me.

No. 299. Grateful Adoration.

1 Before Jehovah's awful throne,
  Ye nations, bow with sacred joy;
  Know that the Lord is God alone;
  He can create, and He destroy.

2 His sovereign power, without our aid,
  Made us of clay, and formed us men;
  And when, like wand'ring sheep, we strayed,
  He brought us to His fold again.

3 We are His people, we His care,
  Our souls and all our mortal frame;
  What lasting honors shall we rear,
  Almighty Maker, to Thy name?

4 We'll crowd Thy gates with thankful songs,
  High as the heavens our voices raise;
  And earth, with her ten thousand tongues,   [praise.
  Shall fill Thy courts with sounding

5 Wide as the world is Thy command,
  Vast as eternity Thy love;
  Firm as a rock Thy truth must stand,
  When rolling years shall cease to move.
                                Rev. Isaac Watts.

No. 300. Praise from All Nations.

1 From all that dwell below the skies,
  Let the Creator's praise arise;
  Let the Redeemer's name be sung
  Through every land, by every tongue.

2 Eternal are Thy mercies, Lord;
  Eternal truth attends Thy word;
  Thy praise shall sound from shore to shore
  Till suns shall rise and set no more.
                                Rev. Isaac Watts.

INDEX OF TITLES.

See page 191 for index of first lines.

Title	No.
A Holy God Worshiped	232
A Lamp and a Light	216
A Land without a Storm	147
A Little Talk with Jesus	117
All Goodness Flows, C. M	236
All People that on Earth	2
Almighty Spirit	181
Almost Persuaded	81
An Open Bible	171
Are You Ready for the Judgment Day?	49
Arise, for Thy Light is Come	13
Art Thou Weary? 8, 5, 8,	100
Ask What I Shall Give	291
A Soldier of the Cross	189
At Jesus' Feet	45
At the Cross	37
Awake, and Sing the Song, S. M	231
Awake, My Soul	285
Awake, My Soul, L. M	271
Azmon, C. M	217
Beautiful, the Little Hands	91
Before the Throne	198
Behold a Stranger, L. M	280
Behold the Bridegroom	127
Beneath His Wings	26
Be Still, O Heart	4
Beulah Land	92
Blessed Assurance	73
Blessed Bible, How I Love It	131
Blessed Name	68
Blest Be the Tie	183
Breathing after Heaven	250
Bright Home	150
Brightly Gleams Our Banner	40
Bringing in the Sheaves	90
Cast Thy Burden	258
Cheer Thee, Sad Soul	82
Child of Sin and Sorrow, 6s and 4s	122
Christ a Pattern	219
Christian Children	290
Christian's Mission	89
Christmas	159
Christmas Evening	218
Christmas Morning, C. M	217
Christ Praised	295
Come, Come to Jesus!	153
Come, Holy Spirit	178
Come, Sacred Spirit!	208
Come, Said Jesus	256
Come, Sinners	182
Come, Thou Almighty King	185
Come, Thou Fount of Every Blessing	151
Come to Jesus; He Will Save You Now	229
Come to the Fountain	108
Come to the Great Physician	32
Come with Rejoicing	39
Consecration Hymn	101
Consolation in Sickness	253
Coronation Song	1
Crown Him	75
Deliverance Will Come	165
Depth of Mercy, 7s	235
Desired of All Nations	225
Desiring to Love	204
Easter Day, L. M	179
Easter Evening	180
Evening Prayer, 8s and 7s	121
Evening Shades, 8s and 7s	102
Eternity is Drawing Nigh	111
Follow All the Way	172
For Ever Here	209
For Those at Sea	112
From Storm Enter Into Rest	131
Gather at the River	70

Title	No.
Gentle Promptings	163
Give Thy Heart to Me	28
God be with You	91
God is Love	294
God is Our Refuge	118
God Speed the Right	146
God's Unspeakable Glory	246
God Will Take Care of You	6
Go Work in My Vineyard	63
Grateful Adoration	299
Grateful Thanks	287
Groaning for the Spirit	274
Hail, Sacred Truth	221
Half Has Never Yet Been Told	52
Hallelujah	170
Happy in Thee	169
Happy Land	16
Hark, My Soul, 7s	289
Hark! What Mean Those Voices? 8s and 7s	233
Hear My Cry	226
Hear the Clink of the Coins	158
Hebron	155
He is Risen	292
He Leadeth Me	298
Herald Angels, 7s	123
Here and Hereafter	132
He Saved Me	81
He Wills	194
Him that Cometh Unto Me	167
His Yoke is Easy	67
Holy! Holy! Lord God Almighty	121
Holy Spirit, Faithful Guide	151
Home of the Soul	165
Hoping for a Revival	260
How Firm a Foundation, 11s	241
Humble Service	222
I am Coming to the Cross	48
I am Praying for You	110
I am Sweeping Through the Gate	99
I Bring My Sins to Thee	112
I'll be There	83
I'll Live for Him	58
I Love to Tell the Story	61
I'm a Pilgrim	115
I Need Thee Every Hour	12
In the Cross of Christ, 8s and 7s	196
In the Royal Army	70
Invocation	197
Invocation	233
Ira Justa Conditoris	210
Is My Name Written There?	17
Israel's Gentle Shepherd	270
I Stretch My Hands to Thee	61
I've Found the Pearl	175
I Will Go	168
Jesus Calls Thee	51
Jesus is Calling	143
Jesus is Mighty to Save	9
Jesus is Mine	115
Jesus is Passing This Way	30
Jesus, My Joy	160
Jesus of Nazareth	85
Jesus of Nazareth Died for Me	22
Jesus Only	58
Jesus, Saviour, Pilot Me	12
Jesus, Victor	161
Jesus, Where'er Thy People Meet, L. M	191
Joy in Heaven	79
Joyous Praises	157
Joy to the World	156
Just as I am, L. M	207
Keep Praying at the Door	149
Lamp of Our Feet	268
Lead, Kindly Light	96

189

INDEX OF TITLES.

Title	No.
Lead Me, Saviour	71
Lebanon, S. M.	228
Let the Children Come	93
Let there be Light	190
Life in His Favor	8
Life's Harvest	88
Life's Raging Billow	279
Like the Fullness of the Sea	141
Longing for Rest	242
Lord, Dismiss Us, 8s and 7s, 6 lines	238
Love Divine, 8s and 7s	107
Love's Sweet Lesson	257
Majestic Sweetness	249
Mean May Seem This House of Clay	186
Mercy	277
More Like Jesus	46
My Cross I've Taken	111
My Faith is Stayed on Thee	25
My Jesus, I Love Thee	77
Nearer the Cross	72
Nearer to Me	87
New Haven, 6s and 4s	210
New Year's Evening	263
New Year's Morning	262
"Ninety and Nine"	230
Not Far from the Kingdom	27
Not Half Has Ever Been Told	166
Nothing but Leaves	56
Nothing but the Blood of Jesus	97
Nothing but the Love of Jesus	18
O, Be Saved!	152
O Could I Speak, C. P. M	202
O Day of Rest and Gladness	187
One Sweetly Solemn Thought	128
On to the Conflict	15
Onward! Christian Soldier	62
Onward! Christian Warriors	19
Open the Book, S. M	261
O Spirit	283
Our Righteousness	243
Pass Me Not	53
Pleading with Thee	174
Praise from All Nations	300
Praise the Lord	7
Praise the Lord, Ye Heavens	173
Praise to the Redeemer	254
Prayer for Guidance	239
Prayer for Pity	286
Prayer for the Spirit	234
Prayer for Union	245
Precious Blood of Calvary	161
Psalm LXXXIV	163
Quæ Stella Sole Pulchrior	215
Redeemed	109
Redeeming Love	21
Redeeming Love	237
Rejoice, and Hail the King	3
Rest in Christ	260
Rest in the Lord	31
Retreat, L. M	213
Returning to God	288
Riches of God's Word	251
Rocked in the Cradle of the Deep	141
Rockingham	176
Rock of Ages, 7s, 6 lines	104
Safe from Every Harm, C. M	212
Safe in the Arms of Jesus	54
Salem's Mighty King	113
Saviour I Look to Thee	211
Scatter Seeds of Kindness	65
Seeking for Me	74
Shepherd of Israel	229
Singing of Jesus	5
Slavery and Death	281
Softly and Tenderly	37
Speak Gently	218
Speed the Tidings	10
Star of Bethlehem	214
Still I am Singing	129
Sun of My Soul	188
Sweet Hour of Prayer	125
Sweet is the Light	177
Take It to the Lord in Prayer	244
Take Me as I Am	78
Teach Me Alway	120
Tell Me the Old, Old Story	47
Tell Us of the Night	290
The Call for Reapers	296
The Christian Farewell	192
The Christian Warfare	153
The Christmas Army	102
The Day is Past	264
The Glory Land	106
The Golden Store	133
The Handwriting on the Wall	86
The Holy Spirit	272
The Home Over There	59
The Inner Calm	207
The Lamb is the Light Thereof	41
The Lily of the Valley	140
The Lord's Courts	236
The Lord's Prayer	118
The Palace of the King	57
The Penitent Pardoned	259
The Pilgrim's Guide	227
There is a Fountain	60
There is a Green Hill Far Away	69
There's a Promise from the Lord	24
There's a Wideness in God's Mercy	80
The Rock of Faith	20
The Rock that is Higher than I	139
The Sins of Men	206
The Soul's Cry Answered, L. M	205
The Spirit in Our Hearts	184
The Story Handed Down	222
The Way, the Truth, the Life	255
This I Did for Thee	98
Thou, Whose Awakening Word	14
Thy Mercies, C. M	284
Thy Will be Done	278
'Tis by the Faith	195
To Jesus I Will Go	126
Tossing on the Billow	130
Trust Him on the Foamy Sea	224
Upon the Waters	100
Vanishing Joys, 8s and 7s	275
Varina, C. M. D	86
Veni Creator Spiritus	273
Verzage Nicht	203
Vision of Dry Bones	207
Walk and Talk with Jesus	20
Watching unto Prayer	265
We'll Work Till Jesus Comes	34
We Long to Move in Thee, C. M	252
We're Marching to Zion	11
We Shall Meet and Rest	270
We Shall Sleep, but Not For Ever	136
What Must it be to be There?	50
What Shall it Profit Me Then?	137
When the King Comes In	95
Where is Thy Refuge?	201
While the Years are Rolling On	110
Whiter than Snow	66
Who is Ready?	23
Will Jesus Find us Watching?	55
Will You Go with Me There?	198
With Christ in Glory	282
With Tearful Eyes	193
Wondrous Love	43
Working for the Lord	81
Ye Must be Born Again	41
Your Mission	149

INDEX OF FIRST LINES.

See page 189 for index of titles.

	No.
A few more struggles here	202
Alas! and did my Saviour bleed?	35
A little talk with Jesus	117
All glory to Jesus be given	9
All hail the pow'r of Jesus' name	1
All people that on earth do dwell	2
Almost persuaded now to believe	84
Am I a soldier of the cross?	189
Angels rejoiced and sweetly sung	217
An open Bible for the world	171
Another six days' work is done	176
Are you ready for the bridegroom?	127
Arise, for thy light is come	13
Arise, my tenderest thoughts, arise	206
Art thou weary, art thou languid?	100
A ruler once came to Jesus by night	41
At the feast of Belshazzar	86
Awake, and sing the song	231
Awake, my soul, stretch every nerve	255
Awake, my soul, to joyful lays	271
Beautiful the little hands	94
Before Jehovah's awful throne	209
Begin the day with God	261
Behold, a stranger's at the door	280
Be still, O heart! why fear and tremble?	4
Blessed assurance, Jesus is mine	73
Blessed Bible, how I love it	134
Blessed stream from Calv'ry's hill	161
Blest be the tie that binds	183
Bright home of our Saviour	150
Brightly gleams our banner	40
Brightness of the Father's glory	245
Brother, you may work for Jesus	89
By cool Siloam's shady rill	219
Called to the feast of the King are we	95
Calm me, my God, and keep me calm	207
Cast thy bread upon the waters	199
Cast thy burden upon the Lord	258
Child of sin and sorrow	122
Christ, the Lord, is risen to-day	232
Come, come to Jesus	153
Come, ev'ry soul by sin oppress'd	229
Come, Holy Ghost, all quickening fire	272
Come, Holy Ghost, our souls inspire	273
Come, Holy Spirit, come	233
Come, Holy Spirit, Heavenly Dove	178
Come, let us join our cheerful songs	217
Come, my soul, thy suit prepare	201
Come, O my soul, in sacred lays	
Come, sacred Spirit, from above	208
Come, said Jesus' sacred voice	256
Come, sinners, to the gospel feast	182
Come, Thou almighty King	185
Come, thou fount of every blessing	151
Come, thou long-expected Jesus	225
Come, walk and talk with Jesus	29
Come, we that love the Lord	11
Come with thy sins to the fountain	108
Depths of mercy, can there be	235
Draw near, O Christ, to me	87
Eternal Father, strong to save	142
Exalt the Lord our God	232
Fade, fade each earthly joy, Jesus is mine	115
Far and near the fields are teeming	206
Far from these scenes of night	106
Father! I stretch my hands to Thee	64
Father of mercies, in Thy word	251
Fear not, O little flock, for He	203
For ever here my rest shall be	209
For ever with the Lord	263
From all that dwell below the skies	300
From ev'ry stormy wind that blows	213
From this bleak hill of storms	131

	No.
God be with you till we meet again	91
God is love; His mercy brightens	294
God is near thee, therefore cheer thee	82
God is the refuge of his saints	148
God loved the world of sinners lost	43
God will take care of you	6
Go work in My vineyard	63
Guide me, O Thou Great Jehovah	227
Hail, sacred truth, whose piercing rays	221
Hail, Thou God of grace and glory	245
Hark, my soul, it is the Lord	289
Hark! the herald angels sing	123
Hark! there comes a whisper	28
Hark! the sound of holy voices	198
Hark! 'tis Christmas Day	157
Hark! what mean those holy voices?	293
Hear the clink of the coins	158
He dies! the friend of sinners dies	180
He leadeth me! oh! blessed thought	298
He, who once in righteous vengeance	240
He wills that I should holy be	194
Holy, Holy, Holy! Lord God Almighty	121
Holy Spirit, faithful Guide	151
Holy Spirit, Teacher Thou	120
Ho! reapers of life's harvest	88
How firm a foundation	241
How lovely are Thy dwellings fair	163
How precious is the book divine	246
I am coming to the cross	48
I am glad; O so glad	170
I am now a child of God	99
I am resting in the Lord	31
I am trusting Him who died for me	26
I bring my sins to Thee	112
If never the gaze of sun and moon	44
If you cannot on the ocean	149
I gave my life for thee	98
I have a Saviour, He's pleading in glory	110
I have heard my Saviour calling	172
I have rend of a beautiful city	166
I know I love Thee better, Lord	52
I know that my Redeemer lives	179
I love to sit at Jesus' feet	45
I love to tell the story	61
I'm a pilgrim, and I'm a stranger	145
I'm helpless, Lord, to Thee I fly	22
In a world so full of weeping	116
I need Thee ev'ry hour	12
In the cross of Christ I glory	196
In the early spring-time	93
In the furrows of thy life	133
In the Royal army	76
I once was a stranger to grace and to God	243
I saw a way-worn trav'ler	165
Is there a heart that is waiting?	30
I've found a friend in Jesus	140
I've found a joy in sorrow	160
I've found the pearl of greatest price	175
I've reached the land of corn and wine	92
I was a wand'ring sheep	228
I was once far away from the Saviour	81
I will go, I cannot stay	168
I will sing you a song	105
Jesus, full of truth and love	260
Jesus, gracious One, calleth now to thee	51
Jesus, I my cross have taken	114
Jesus is tenderly calling thee home	143
Jesus, my Lord, to Thee I cry	78
Jesus, my Saviour, to Bethlehem came	71
Jesus, my strength, my hope	265
Jesus, Saviour, pilot me	42
Jesus, where'er Thy people meet	191
Jesus, while our hearts are bleeding	278
Joy to the world	156
Just as I am, without one plea	297

INDEX OF FIRST LINES.

	No.
Keep praying at the door	119
Lamp of our feet whereby we trace	268
Lead, kindly Light, amid th' encircling	16
Lead us, Heavenly Father, lead us	230
Let children hear the mighty deeds	222
Let us gather up the sunbeams	65
Life in His favor! Forgiven all sin	8
Life is but a fleeting dream	132
Listen to the blessed invitation	107
Listen to the gentle promptings	103
Look down, O Lord, with pitying eye	207
Look, ye saints, the sight is glorious	75
Lord, dismiss us with Thy blessing	238
Lord, I care not for riches	17
Lord Jesus, I long to be perfectly whole	66
Love divine, all love excelling	107
Marching, marching, like a mighty army	162
Mercy, O Thou Son of David	277
More like Jesus would I be	46
My faith is stayed on Thee	25
My faith looks up to Thee	210
My Jesus I love Thee	77
My life, my love I give to Thee	58
My soul is rejoicing and sweet is my song	169
Nearer the cross my heart can say	72
New every morning is Thy love	155
No mortal can with Him compare	219
Not far from the kingdom	27
Nothing but leaves	56
Nothing but the love of Jesus	18
Now begin the heavenly theme	237
Now, from the altar of our hearts	287
Now to heav'n our pray'r ascending	146
O, could I speak the matchless worth	202
O daughter, take good heed	57
O day of rest and gladness	187
O for a sweet inspiring ray	282
O for the happy hour	234
O had I, my Saviour, the wings of a dove	242
Oh, for a thousand tongues to sing	68
Oh, land of rest for thee I sigh	34
Oh, praise the Lord, sing to His name	7
Oh, think of the home over there	59
O little town of Bethlehem	159
O love divine, how sweet thou art	204
O mean may seem this house of clay	186
One sweetly solemn thought	128
On the Rock of faith I am building	20
Onward, Christian soldier	62
Onward! O Christian warriors	10
O, sing of Jesus, "Lamb of God"	169
O, sometimes the shadows are deep	139
O Spirit of the living God	283
O Thou from whom all goodness	236
O Thou whose tender mercy hears	288
Our Father, who art in heaven	118
Our Lord is now ascended	161
O, we are volunteers in the army	125
O weary burdened souls opprest	32
Pass me not, O gentle Saviour	53
Plunged in a gulf of dark despair	254
Praise the Lord! ye heavens adore Him	173
Pray, brethren, pray	111
Preserved by Thine almighty arm	212
Rejoice, and hail the King	3
Return, O God of love, return	250
Rocked in the cradle of the deep	144
Rock of Ages, cleft for me	101
Safe in the arms of Jesus	54
Saviour! breathe an evening blessing	121
Saviour, I look to Thee	244
Saviour, lead me lest I stray	71
Saviour, teach me day by day	257
Saviour! visit Thy plantation	167

	No.
Say, where is thy refuge, my brother?	201
Scorn not the slightest word or deed	223
See Israel's gentle Shepherd stand	270
Shall we gather at the river?	70
Shepherd of Israel, from above	220
Show pity, Lord! O Lord, forgive	205
Silently the shades of evening	102
Singing of Jesus all the way along	5
Sing to the Lord, to God our Father	39
Sinner, how thy heart is troubled	152
Slavery and death the cup contains	281
Softly and tenderly, Jesus is calling	37
Son of David, hear my cry	226
Sovereign Ruler, Lord of all	259
Sowing in the morning	90
Speak gently! It is better far	218
Speed the tidings o'er the ocean	19
Still I am singing, Jesus, of Thee	120
Strew the way with palm leaves	113
Sun of my soul, Thou Saviour dear	188
Sweet hour of prayer, sweet hour of prayer	125
Sweet is the light of Sabbath eve	177
Sweet to look inward, and attend	253
Take my life, and let it be	101
Tell the Old, Old story	47
The day is past and gone	264
The Lord is my Shepherd, I shall not want	67
There is a fountain filled with blood	60
There is a green hill far away	69
There is a happy land	16
There is a land of pure delight	36, 83
There is joy among the angels	79
There's a fullness in God's mercy	141
There's a gentle voice within calls away	126
There's a great day coming	49
There's a promise from the Lord	24
There's a wideness in God's mercy	80
There were ninety and nine that safely lay	230
The Saviour's workers are in line	33
The Spirit, in our hearts	184
Thou art the way! To Thee alone	255
Thou, whose almighty Word	190
Thou, whose awakening word	14
Thy presence, everlasting God	162
'Tis by the fall of joys to come	185
To Christ our Lord and faithful friend	21
Tossed upon life's raging billow	279
Tossing on the billow	130
To Thee, my God, whose presence fills	286
To Thy temple I repair	236
Trav'ler, whither art thou going?	147
Trust in God for every blessing	224
Vain are all terrestrial pleasures	275
Watchman! tell us of the night	290
We are little Christian children	200
Weary, oh, yes, thou art weary	174
We have taken up our stand	15
We long to move and breathe in Thee	252
We shall sleep, but not for ever	136
We speak of the land of the blest	50
What a friend we have in Jesus	214
What can wash away my stain?	97
What means this eager, anxious throng?	85
What shall it profit me by and by?	137
What star is this, with beams so bright?	215
What tho' clouds are hov'ring o'er me	38
When all Thy mercies, O my God	281
When Jesus comes to reward his servants	55
When marshalled on the nightly plain	211
When shall I hear the inward voice?	274
Where the faded flow'r shall freshen	276
While I to grief my soul gave way	209
While shepherds watched their flocks	218
Who but Thou, almighty Spirit	181
Who is ready, who is willing	23
Why speed so quickly, O Pilgrim?	138
With tearful eyes I look around	193

www.ingramcontent.com/pod-product-compliance
Lightning Source LLC
Chambersburg PA
CBHW032137160426
43197CB00008B/673